WITHDRAWN

MIRACLE IN KOREA

Troops from the 3d Infantry Division's 65th Infantry Regiment depart the Hungnam beachhead on a Navy LSU (Landing Ship, Utility). U.S. Army Photo 111–SC–370636, courtesy of National Archives.

MIRACLE IN KOREA

*The Evacuation of X Corps
from the Hungnam Beachhead*

By GLENN C. COWART

University of South Carolina Press

Copyright © 1992 University of South Carolina

Published in Columbia, South Carolina, by the
University of South Carolina Press

Manufactured in the United States of America

Library of Congress Cataloging-in-Publication Data

Cowart, Glenn C., 1930–
   Miracle in Korea : the evacuation of X Corps from the Hungnam
beachhead / by Glenn C. Cowart.
     p. cm.
   Includes bibliographical references (p.) and index.
   ISBN 0-87249-829-8 (hard cover : acid-free)
   1. Korean War, 1950–1953—Campaigns—Korea (North)—Changjin
Reservoir. 2. Changjin Reservoir (Korea)—History. 3. United
States. Army. Infantry Division, 3rd—History. 4. Korean War,
1950–1953—Regimental histories—United States. I. Title.
DS918.2.C35C69   1992
951.904′2—dc20   92-11610

For my children,
Paul, Diane and David

Contents

Illustrations	ix
Tables	xi
Maps	xiii
Preface	xv
Acknowledgments	xxi
Abbreviations	xxv
Chronology	xxxi
Introduction	1
1. Land of the Morning Calm	9
2. War on a Shoestring	15
3. Prelude to Combat	21
4. Problems in Communications	33
5. Guerrilla Warfare	39
6. The Chinese Intervene	51
7. Into the Abyss	61
8. Trading Space for Time	75
9. Deliverance	89
Retrospect	101
Appendix A	
Strength Figures for the 3d Infantry Division on Selected Dates	111
Appendix B	
A Brief History of the 3d Infantry Division	123
Bibliography	127
Index	131

Illustrations

Frontispiece

Troops depart the Hungnam beachhead.

Following page 26

M–46 tanks from the 3d Infantry Division's 64th Heavy Tank Battalion.

155mm howitzer in action.

Captured Russian SU–76 self-propelled guns.

Vehicles await loading in Hungnam harbor.

An Army M–19 self-propelled gun carriage.

The destruction of a railroad viaduct in North Korea.

Soldiers boarding the USNS *General H. B. Freeman*.

Troops wade out to waiting landing craft.

Following page 82

Major General Edward M. Almond, Captain Alexander M. Haig and 1st Lieutenant Robert J. St. Aubin.

Major General Edward M. Almond, Major General Robert H. Soule and Brigadier General Armistead D. Mead.

Explosives being unloaded on the dock at Hungnam.

Smoke billows as troops withdraw from Hungnam.

USS *Begor* passes as huge explosions rip the harbor installations at Hungnam.

Major General Robert H. Soule.

TABLES

1. Authorized Personnel Strength for Divisional Units — 4

2. Frequency Overlaps in Megacycles — FM Radios — 36

3. Organization of XIII Army Group, Chinese Communist Forces — 56

4. Organization of IX Army Group, Chinese Communist Forces — 57

5. Troop Strength of Infantry Battalions — Dec. 24, 1950 — 91

A.1. 3d Infantry Division Authorized and Actual Strength Figures — August 23, 1950 — 111

A.2. 3d Infantry Division Authorized and Actual Strength Figures — November 23, 1950 — 115

A.3. 3d Infantry Division Authorized and Actual Strength Figures — December 24, 1950 — 119

Maps

1.	Southeast Asia	2
2.	The Korean Peninsula	6
3.	Road Distances in Northeast Korea (in miles)—1950 Roadnet	10
4.	3d Infantry Division Situation Map, Nov. 11–24, 1950	44
5.	3d Infantry Division Situation Map, Nov. 25–30, 1950	48
6.	3d Infantry Division Situation Map, Dec. 1–4, 1950	64
7.	3d Infantry Division Situation Map, Dec. 5–10, 1950	69
8.	3d Infantry Division Situation Map, Dec. 11–16, 1950	74
9.	3d Infantry Division Situation Map, Dec. 17–22, 1950	78
10.	Northeast Korea, Phase Lines at Hungnam	84
11.	Hungnam, North Korea—Beach Areas Used in Evacuation	93

PREFACE

Almost forty years have passed since the guns fell silent in Korea. We have added roughly ninety-eight millions to our population—indeed, less than half of our present citizens were alive during that war—and we have lived through the trauma of Vietnam.

These circumstances tend to obscure the fact that, as in Vietnam, we fought an earlier war in which the United States, for reasons valid at the time, chose to settle for stalemate rather than victory.

A number of excellent books have been written on the Korean War in recent years. This account concerns itself with one specific campaign: the evacuation of the beachhead at Hungnam in northeast Korea by the U.S. Tenth Corps (hereinafter X Corps) in November and December of 1950.

The purpose of this narrative is to tell the story, as factually as possible, of what happened to one infantry division in its baptism of fire. The campaign that ensued did not begin or end the conflict nor did it win or lose the war. It was important only in that it allowed a large number of United Nations forces to escape entrapment and to fight another day with a newfound confidence. It proved that the American soldier could stand up to the hordes of Chinese Communist troops whose leaders were quite willing to sustain huge losses in order to prevail.

The development of a group of men into a cohesive fighting unit does not happen overnight, and two months is not an adequate period in which to accomplish this goal. But sixty days were all that could be allotted to the 3d Infantry Division if the Korean War was to be brought to a successful conclusion in the fall of 1950, before the bitter Korean winter set in.[1]

The American military establishment had been stretched to the breaking point by the decision to intervene in the Korean War. As General Omar Bradley so aptly stated, it was "the wrong war, at the wrong time, in the wrong place, and against the wrong enemy."[2] But once a shooting war is started, events have a way of wresting control from humans and becoming in effect the master rather than the servant.

A major factor in saving the United States from an embarrassing defeat in Korea was its unchallenged control of the air above and the seas around the war-torn peninsula. Euphoria over the effectiveness of air power in World War II misled the American people and their leaders into believing that ground forces would play a limited role in any future conflict.

Because it significantly affected every decision made in the military operations in northeast Korea, the weather factor almost deserves a book of its own. That Korean winter of 1950 will remain forever in the memory of every American who fought there. The cold was so severe that one's body seemed to go into shock. The thought processes were slowed, and any part of the body exposed to the elements, especially nose, ears, hands, and feet, actually hurt from the cold. Gloves were helpful, but only mittens kept the fingers warm.

Hypothermia was a medically unknown or little-understood condition in 1950. Yet we now know that dehydration and lack of proper food can contribute to loss of body heat. This can lead to an insufficient oxygen supply to the brain which, in turn, can impair the mind as well as physical functions. And ultimately it can lead to death.

So much energy was expended providing body heat that such simple activities as digging, walking, or just standing became acts of exertion. Failure to move about could result in frostbite, especially on the extremities; yet movement caused pain, and to march any distance on numb feet was a test of endurance.

Hunger often was not satisfied by field rations. Sweets, because they produced energy, were craved for, and the desire for hot, sweet liquids such as hot chocolate was a constant fantasy.

Nor were problems confined to the human body. Malfunctioning weapons were the rule rather than the exception, until the troops learned to clean them more often and to forgo the application of oil to the moving parts, a standard procedure in warmer climes. Up in the mountains near Sachang-ni, where it was at least twenty degrees colder than in the lower elevations, some units were dismayed when the sub-freezing temperatures caused the firing tubes of the 4.2" mortars to split. Artillery shells fell short of their targets and radio equipment was effective only over limited distances.

The movement of tanks and trucks over roads made slick by ice and snow was increasingly dangerous as stalled and overturned vehicles impeded the men and equipment on roads meant for ox-carts.

The weather also played havoc with tactical air support. All operations were hampered, but carrier based aircraft felt the greatest impact due to the increased hazards of snow, ice, rough seas and surface fog for carrier takeoffs and landings. Missions utilizing land-based aircraft were also curtailed, but Air Force transports and Army light aircraft used in directing artillery fire continued to airlift items such as ammunition, rations, sleeping bags and blankets and, equally important, to evacuate the seriously wounded.

An unkind fate decreed that I live through most of this story and travel the road from Wonsan to Hamhung and Hungnam. Unfortunately, or perhaps fortunately, I did not go north of Hamhung.

I can, however, vouch for the accuracy of historian Barrie Pitt's words when he wrote that "adrenalin flows faster in the veins of tired men escaping a trap than it does in those of tired men trying to close it."[3]

One of the great frustrations of ground combat is something called battlefield isolation. A soldier's perception of the battle is limited to what he can see and hear with perhaps a smattering of information coming over his unit's radio and telephone-net. It is this ignorance of the overall picture that often breeds fear and confusion.

The suddenness with which the Inchon landing turned a defensive war into an offensive one caught the U.S. Army with a limited availability of maps of North Korea. Tactical maps of 1:25,000 scale were not available, and leaders relied on less detailed 1:50,000 maps prepared by the Japanese army, based on 1916 data. As a result, unit commanders never felt totally confident regarding terrain features depicted on the maps and what was actually awaiting them on the ground just ahead.[4]

Cold, confusion, poor maps, primitive roads and malfunctioning weapons; this is what awaited the 3d Infantry Division as it prepared to deploy in Korea.

Notes

1. At the time of the 3d Infantry Division's arrival in Korea, there was a widespread belief in Tokyo and Washington that the war was entering its final phase. In this scenario the division's primary role was seen to be one of occupation duty in North Korea until such time as a political solution could be achieved. See also note 3, chapter 2.

2. General of the Army Omar N. Bradley, Chairman of the Joint Chiefs of Staff; testimony before joint House-Senate committees (Armed Services/Foreign Relations) investigating the relief of General of the Army Douglas MacArthur. 82nd Congress, 1st Session, 1951.

3. Barrie Pitt: *Churchill and the Generals*, Bantam Books, 1981

4. Maps used in preparing this manuscript were taken from Army Map Series L751—Korea: 1:50,000 Grids 6631, 6632, 6633, 6634, 6635, 6731, 6732, 6733, and 6734 (Sheets I, II, III, IV for most grids). Maps included in the text were based on Army Map Series L551—Korea: 1:250,000, courtesy of the National Archives and Army Map Service.

ACKNOWLEDGMENTS

Any attempt to write a history of this sort must, of necessity, be a partnership. The willingness of many to share their memories and personal papers, and to devote time to answer questions made it all possible.

Forty years is a sizable span in a lifetime, and it is understandable that the ability to recall events of long ago may be difficult. Some men remembered as if it were yesterday, while others had difficulty in reaching that far back in time. However, the warmth and enthusiasm with which I was uniformly received by comrades old and new made the endeavor worthwhile.

I must begin by acknowledging my debt to T. R. Fehrenbach, whose moving narrative *This Kind of War* planted the seed that bore fruit in the completion of this manuscript. And I must express my gratitude to Lieutenant Colonel Roy E. Appleman, USA (Ret.), the premier military historian of our time, for his willingness to share advice and guidance. No study of the Korean War would be complete without reference to his detailed narratives of this conflict.

Those who so generously shared their time and memories include:

Major General John S. Guthrie and Brigadier General William W. Harris, commanders during the Hungnam operation of the 7th and 65th Infantry regiments, respectively;

Brigadier General James O. Boswell, the 7th Infantry's executive officer (and later regimental commander), whose insights on the Hungnam operation were invaluable;

Lieutenant General Pat W. Crizer and Brigadier General Harley F. Mooney, whose perspective of the fighting from a platoon leader/company commander's viewpoint and whose grasp of infantry organization and tactics were essential to the accuracy of the narrative;

Brigadier General Robert M. Blanchard, Colonel Samuel G. Kail, and Colonel Howard B. St. Clair, battalion commanders in the 15th, 7th and 65th Infantry, respectively, at the time of the action described, and whose memories helped me re-create much of the battle scene;

Colonels C. J. "Mike" Molloy and William H. Nolph, my former company commanders, who by their example instilled in me a deep respect for those who chose the military as a lifetime career;

and Major Joseph J. Piaseczny, communications officer in the 7th Infantry at Hungnam, who shared with me his considerable knowledge of the complex subject of battlefield communications.

A special word of thanks is also due to General Matthew B. Ridgway, one of America's greatest battlefield commanders of this century, for his warm words of encouragement; and to General (then Lieutenant Colonel) Fred C. Weyand, whose electric guitar playing in the division CP (command post) at Wonsan for an audience of one on a cold November night probably gave me the distinction of being the only sergeant ever to be serenaded by a future army chief of staff.

    I am also indebted to Major James S. Day of the West Point academic staff for his review of the preliminary version of this manuscript. His incisive comments and recommendations greatly improved the narrative. And, most important, I must express my deepest appreciation to my wife, Shirley, for her support and encouragement to see the project through.

Abbreviations

ADC	Assistant division commander. Also, Aide-de-Camp; a duty assignment as assistant to a General officer; rank depends on General officer's rank.
AT	Anti-tank artillery shell normally used against enemy armored formations. Also see HEAT.
BCT	Battalion combat team. An infantry battalion plus supporting arms (artillery, armor, engineers) as required by the mission assigned.
BG	Brigadier general, one-star rank (usually an assistant division commander, or CG, division artillery).
Bn	Battalion (infantry, artillery, armored, engineer). (3d Bn, 7th Infantry Regt or 3/7th Infantry) (39th Field Artillery Bn or 39th F/A) (64th Heavy Tank Bn or 64th Tank Bn).
Bty	Firing battery, Field Artillery.
CCF	Chinese Communist Forces (also known as Peoples Liberation Army).
CG	Commanding general of a division, corps or army.

Co	Company of infantry, armor, engineers, etc.
C/O	Commanding officer of a unit from company up to regimental level.
COL	Colonel (usually a regimental commander or staff officer at division or higher headquarters).
Corps	A tactical grouping of two or more divisions; identified with a Roman numeral (I Corps, X Corps). Two or more corps constitute an army.
CP	Command post. A headquarters location.
CPT	Captain (usually a company or battery commander; also a battalion staff officer).
Div	An infantry division (i.e., 3d Infantry Division).
DivArty	A headquarters exercising command over the artillery battalions organic to an infantry division; commanded by a brigadier general who reports to the division commander.
EM	Enlisted man (men). Basic soldier with rank of private to master sergeant.
EUSAK	Eight United States Army, Korea
F/A	Field artillery (usually an artillery battalion).

1LT	First lieutenant (usually a platoon leader).
FAC	Forward air controller. Generally an Air Force officer assigned to an infantry unit in a liaison capacity for the purpose of coordinating air strikes in support of ground combat activity.
FO	Forward observer. Generally an artillery officer assigned to an infantry unit in a liaison capacity for the purpose of coordinating artillery fire in support of combat activity.
GEN	General, four-star rank. (Usually an army commander).
G–1/S–1	Personnel officer at army, corps, division (G); regimental or battalion level (S).
G–2/S–2	Intelligence officer at army, corps, division (G); regimental or battalion level (S).
G–3/S–3	Operations and training officer at army, corps, division (G); regimental or battalion level (S).
G–4/S–4	Supply officer at army, corps, division (G); regimental or battalion level (S).
HE	High explosive artillery shell normally used against enemy troop formations.
HEAT	High explosive anti-tank shell used against armor.

Hq	Headquarters of an army, corps, division, regiment, battalion, company or battery.
KATUSA	Korean Augmentation to the United States Army. Korean nationals who were impressed into military service and given a modicum of military training in Japan. Most were returned to the ROK Army; however, some were retained by U.S. Army units as translators.
LTC	Lieutenant colonel (usually a battalion commander, regimental X/O or division staff officer).
LTG	Lieutenant general, three-star rank (usually a corps commander).
MAJ	Major (usually a battalion executive officer or regimental staff officer).
MG	Major general, two-star rank (usually a division commander).
MLR	Main line of resistance. A defined position from which an infantry unit will make its main effort to resist an attacking enemy force, i.e: the front line.
MSR	Main supply route. A road or series of roads over which troops and supplies can be moved in support of combat operations.
NKPA	North Korean Peoples Army.

Off	Commissioned officer from 2d lieutenant to four star general; has command authority.
OPLR	Outpost line of resistance. A series of manned positions (foxholes) from which warnings of an enemy advance are received. Troops manning such positions are ordered back to the MLR when an attack is imminent.
PLA	Peoples Liberation Army. Name used by CCF to disguise the presence of regular CCF units in Korea.
Plt	Platoon. A unit consisting of two or more squads.
Plt Ldr	Platoon Leader (usually a 1st or 2d Lieutenant).
RCT	Regimental combat team. An infantry regiment plus supporting arms (artillery, armor, engineers) as required by the mission assigned.
Regt	An infantry regiment (i.e., 7th Infantry).
ROK	Republic of Korea (South Korea).
2LT	Second lieutenant (usually a platoon leader).
Sec	Section. A tactical group larger than a squad but smaller than a platoon, used for crew-served weapons (mortars, recoilless rifles, machine guns).

Sqd	Squad. The smallest tactical group in an (army) infantry unit consisting of nine enlisted men (1950).
Sqd Ldr	Squad Leader. Senior noncommissioned officer in charge of a squad.
Svc	Service battery, Field Artillery.
T/O&E	Table of Organization and Equipment. A Department of the Army publication promulgating the mission of a subordinate unit, its organizational structure and allowances in manpower and matériel.
UN	United Nations.
US	United States of America.
USA	United States Army.
USAF	United States Air Force.
USMC	United States Marine Corps.
USN	United States Navy.
WO	Warrant Officer. A specialist in an administrative or technical assignment; has supervisory control but no command authority.
WP	White phosporous artillery shell capable of inflicting severe burns on enemy personnel.
X/O	Executive officer of a unit from company to regimental level.

Chronology

June 25, 1950	North Korean forces attack South Korean (ROK) Army positions south of 38th parallel in predawn strike.
June 27	President Truman orders U.S. air and naval forces to provide assistance to South Korea. UN Security Council calls on member nations to aid in repelling aggressors.
June 29	Seoul, capital of South Korea, occupied by North Korean army.
June 30	Truman commits U.S. ground forces to combat role in Korea. Air and naval forces authorized to strike military targets in North Korea.
July 1–2	1st Bn, 21st Infantry, (Task Force Smith) arrives in Korea by airlift from Japan.
July 5	U.S. troops fail to stop North Korean armor and infantry at Osan; remainder of 24th Infantry Division arrives in Korea. Delaying action withdrawals begin.

July 14	25th Infantry Division arrives in Korea.
July 15	North Korean forces cross Kum River.
July 18	Elements of U.S. 1st Cavalry Division arrive in Korea.
July 20	24th Infantry Division forced to abandon Taejon; division commander (General William F. Dean) missing in action.
July 31	2d Infantry Division arrives in Korea from Fort Lewis, WA. 5th Regimental Combat Team arrives from Hawaii.
August 3	1st Marine Brigade (Provisional) arrives in Korea from Camp Pendelton, CA.
August 4	NPKA forces repulsed in attack on U.S./ROK forces in positions protecting Pusan.
August 8	North Koreans breach Naktong River line.
August 15	UN troops repel attacks at Naktong River.
August 30	3d Infantry Division departs San Francisco enroute to Japan.
September 1–5	NKPA forces make repeated attempts to break through U.N.

	positions at Naktong. General Walker shuttles units to plug weak spots.
September 15	U.S. X Corps (1st Marine and 7th Infantry divisions) execute surprise amphibious assault at Inchon.
September 18	U.S. forces in Pusan perimeter push north in counteroffensive operations designed to link up with elements of X Corps now moving rapidly inland to cut NKPA lines of retreat.
September 25	U.S. Joint Chiefs of Staff authorize use of American military forces north of 38th parallel.
September 26	Seoul recaptured by elements of X Corps.
October 1	South Korean troops cross 38th parallel.
October 9	U.S. troops cross 38th parallel.
October 13–14	First CCF troop units cross the Yalu River into North Korea.
October 15	President Truman and General MacArthur meet at Wake Island.
October 19	Pyongyang, capital of North Korea, falls to U.S. Eighth Army.

October 26	CCF troops ambush 7th Regiment, 6th ROK Division, at Onjang. ROK troops retreat in panic, suffering heavy losses in men and matériel.
October 26	1st Marine Division lands at Wonsan.
November 1–2	CCF ambushes 1st Cavalry Division at Unsan.
November 8	Eighth Army makes stand on south bank of Chongchon; CCF forces withdraw from contact with U.N. forces.
November 11–20	3d Infantry Division lands at Wonsan on east coast of North Korea.
November 21	Elements of 17th Infantry (7th Infantry Division) reach Yalu River at Hyesanjin.
November 24	Eighth Army resumes offensive operations designed to bring an end to the fighting.
November 25–30	CCF Second Phase Offensive launched, causing confusion and heavy casualties among 2d and 25th Infantry divisions.
November 27	X Corps resumes offensive.
December 1	CCF annihilates elements of 7th Infantry Division (Task Force Faith) east of Chosin Reservoir.

December 1	U.N. forces begin retreat southward.
December 5	Chinese forces occupy Pyongyang.
December 7	U.S. Marines begin epic withdrawal from Yudam-ni in effort to escape entrapment.
December 9	Wonsan evacuated. Port facilities demolished.
December 10	3d Division task force (Task Force Dog) fights north to Chinhung-ni, joins forces with 1st Marine Division.
December 11	Marine division begins outloading on ships in Hungnam harbor.
December 19	7th Infantry Division completes outloading at Hungnam; 3d Infantry Division assumes responsibility for defending the beachhead.
December 23	General Walker, Eighth Army commander, killed in jeep-truck accident.
December 24	3d Infantry Division completes evacuation of X Corps at Hungnam. Port facilities demolished. Chinese forces reach 38th parallel.

MIRACLE IN KOREA

Introduction

Theory does not win wars. And it was in theory only that the army infantry divisions sent to fight in Korea were structured along the same organizational lines that had been adopted by the army on the eve of World War II.

At full strength a division was composed of three infantry regiments, five field artillery battalions, a heavy tank battalion and specialized service units such as signal, engineer, ordnance, medical, quartermaster, reconnaissance and military police (see Table 1).

The infantry regiments had three battalions, each composed of three rifle companies and a heavy-weapons company. The rifle companies had three rifle platoons and a weapons platoon armed with 60mm mortars and 57mm recoilless rifles. The heavy-weapons company was equipped with the more powerful 81mm mortars, 75mm recoilless rifles and heavy machine guns.[1]

Each of the three 105mm artillery battalions had three firing batteries and a service battery (a total of eighteen guns). There was one 155mm artillery battalion (also eighteen guns) and an anti-aircraft (automatic weapons) battalion.

In addition to the divisional heavy tank battalion

MAP No. 1 - Southeast Asia (Courtesy of Army Map Service, Corps of Engineers, U.S. Army)

(71 tanks), each infantry regiment had an organic tank company of 22 tanks for a divisional total of 149 tanks.

In theory, then, the firepower that could be generated by an infantry division, fully manned and equipped, was awesome. Besides the tanks and artillery pieces, the so-called crew-served weapons (i.e., 60mm and 81mm mortars and 57mm and 75mm recoilless rifles) in the infantry battalions, plus the 4.2" mortars in the regimental Heavy Mortar companies represented a tremendous potential that could be brought to bear on an enemy position. Although the tactical situation often made it impossible to coordinate all units and weapons in true textbook fashion, the flexibility for attaching one or more elements of the division to a particular command for specific engagements promoted effective use of the resources at hand.

No armored or airborne divisions were employed in Korea; however, the 187th Airborne Regimental Combat Team (basically a parachute infantry regiment with attached artillery and other supporting troops) did see action.

The infantry does not fight alone, and anyone who has ever served as an infantryman would be quick to acknowledge this fact. The combat arms (infantry, armor, artillery) are supported by the efforts of many. The engineers with their road-building skills and equipment for bridging rivers and deep gullies; ordnance troops with their expertise in repairing and maintaining weapons and vehicles; the quartermaster personnel with their ability to provide an uninterrupted flow of ammunition, food, water, and clothing; the sol-

Table 1
AUTHORIZED PERSONNEL STRENGTH FOR DIVISIONAL UNITS (1950)

	Officers	Warrant Officers	Enlisted Men
Infantry Division	958	49	17,797
Infantry Regiment	156	4	3,614
Infantry Battalion	34	0	883
Infantry Rifle Company	6	0	205
Infantry Weapons Company	5	0	160
Infantry Rifle Platoon	1	0	38
Infantry Rifle Squad	0	0	9
Artillery Battalion	46	2	621
Artillery Firing Battery	8	0	131
Artillery Service Battery	3	1	81
Heavy Tank Battalion	36	3	638
Engineer Combat Battalion	42	3	927
Medical Battalion	46	2	293
Signal Company	12	3	354
Ordnance Maintenance Company	15	4	302
Quartermaster Company	12	0	248
Military Police Company	7	0	180
Reconnaissance Company	6	0	164

Source: T/O&E 7N Infantry Division (1948)

diers who provide motor transport to move the supplies and troops who will use them; signal corpsmen with their critical role of providing reliable signal/communications gear; the medical personnel to treat and evacuate the wounded—all of these needs are met with the assignment of service or support units to the modern infantry division.

And just as the lack of adequately trained infantrymen can diminish the combat effectiveness of the division, so can the lack of supporting troop units adversely affect the infantryman's ability to get his job done.

In mid-1950, the American military establishment was woefully understrength. Budget cuts in fiscal 1949 and 1950 resulted in manpower shortages, particularly in the army and navy. With the exception of the 1st Infantry Division on occupation duty in Germany and the 82d Airborne Division at Fort Bragg, North Carolina, no combat unit was up to its wartime allocation in personnel or equipment.

President Truman's decision to intervene when the North Koreans invaded South Korea was bold and necessary if communism was to be contained. In the first weeks after doing so, it also appeared to have been foolhardy.

The average American soldier in 1950 was the product of a peacetime army in which discipline and training were neglected. One young officer remembered "a lackadaisical attitude at Fort Devens, Massachusetts, in common with other army posts. Training was given a lower priority than fatigue details and policing the area. The senior officers seemed to be basking in the afterglow of their World War II success and didn't expect to have to fight another war so soon after the big one."[2]

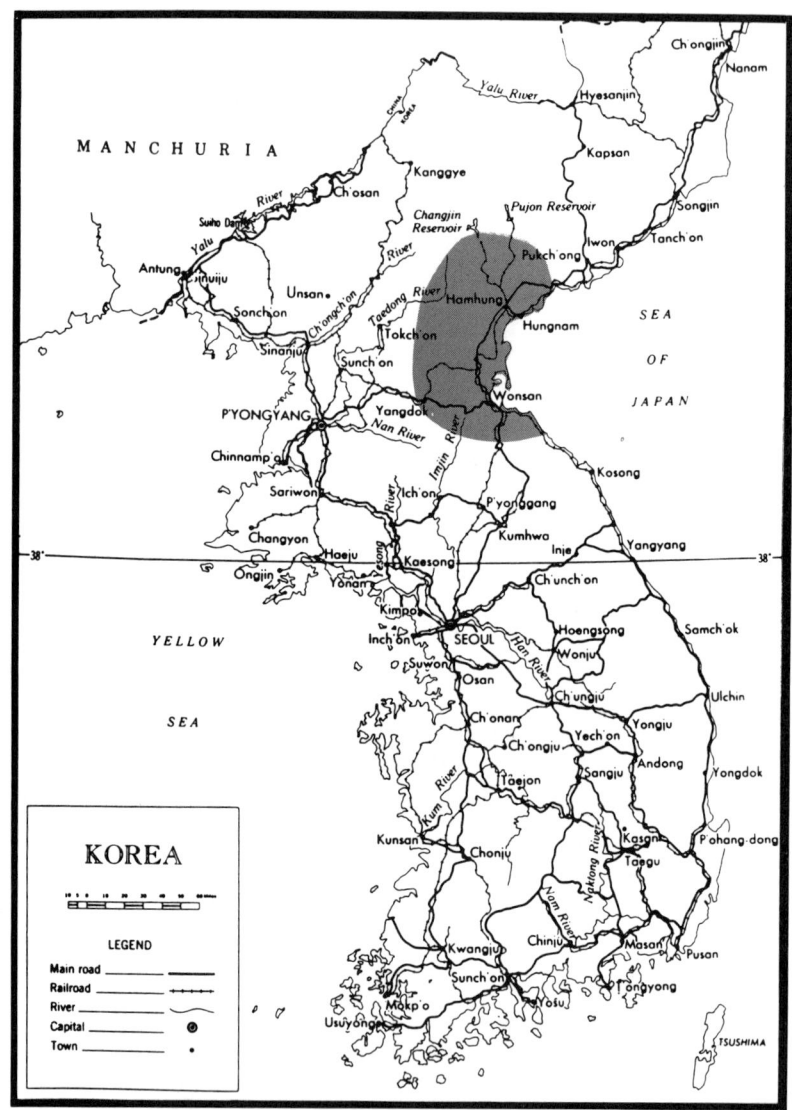

MAP No. 2 - The Korean Peninsula. Shaded area identifies the operational zone of the 3d Infantry Division in North Korea from November 11 to December 24, 1950. (Courtesy of Army Map Service, Corps of Engineers, U.S. Army)

Introduction 7

The basic training cycle for army recruits had been reduced from fourteen weeks to eight. Bayonet training, thought to be too dangerous, had been eliminated, and it was a rare instance in which the new soldier fired more than two hundred rounds with his primary weapon.

After basic, assignment to Europe was a near impossibility, since many of the soldiers in Germany reenlisted to fill their own vacancies. This meant that the majority of young Americans coming out of the pipeline ended up in assignments on a Pacific atoll or, if lucky, the Japanese mainland, where garrison duty was anything but strenuous. Houseboys kept boots and barracks spotless and there were plenty of geisha girls with whom to drink beer. Whatever combat skills had been learned in basic training were quickly forgotten in the comforts of a peacetime billet.

The Eighth United States Army on occupation duty in Japan consisted of the 7th, 24th, and 25th Infantry Divisions and the 1st Cavalry Division (at that time structured as an infantry unit). All were at 60 to 70 percent of their full T/O&E (Table of Organization and Equipment) strength, regimental tank companies having been deleted.

Much of their supplies and equipment, particularly ammunition and radio equipment left over from World War II, was defective or unserviceable. The bad ammo was soon fired or dumped; the radios, with outdated batteries, malfunctioned as cold weather set in.

These Japan-based divisions were the first units committed to ground combat when President Truman gave the order to send troops to Korea.

Notes

1. Total armament for a fully equipped infantry battalion (three rifle companies and a weapons company) in 1950 was:

534 Rifle, caliber .30 M1
253 Carbine, caliber .30
130 Pistol, automatic, caliber .45
  45 Automatic rifle, caliber .30
  13 Machine gun, caliber .30 (air cooled)
   4 Machine gun, caliber .30 (water cooled)
   8 Machine gun, caliber .30
   9 Mortar, 60mm
   4 Mortar, 81mm
   9 Recoilless rifle, 57mm
   4 Recoilless rifle, 75mm
   9 Rocket launcher, 2.36"
  11 Rocket launcher, 3.5"

The 2.36" rocket launcher, which proved ineffective in Korea against the Russian-built T–34 tank, was quickly replaced with the 3.5" version. Source: T/O&E 7 11N Infantry Regiment (1948).

2. Author interview: LTG Pat W. Crizer, USA (Ret.), June 3, 1989.

1
LAND OF THE MORNING CALM

Eighty miles north of the 38th parallel and approximately one hundred miles due east of Pyongyang is the city of Wonsan.[1] Situated in the southwest corner of Yonghung Bay on North Korea's east coast, it is one of the peninsula's best natural harbors. It is also the eastern terminus of one of the few east-west highways in that mountainous country.

Here the Taebaek Mountains come down almost to the sea, with the coastal plain extending not more than ten miles inland. A primitive road and a rail line ran along the seaward base of the mountains, connecting Wonsan with Hamhung, sixty-nine miles to the north, and Pusan, far to the south.

Twenty-two miles inland from Wonsan, the village of Majon-ni was also of strategic importance to the contending military forces, since it was situated at the headwaters of the river Imjin and was the site of a road junction with highways leading east to Wonsan, west to Pyongyang and south to Seoul.

It was along this shelf-like road from Wonsan to Majon-ni, with its deep gorges and hairpin turns twisting precariously through a three-thousand-

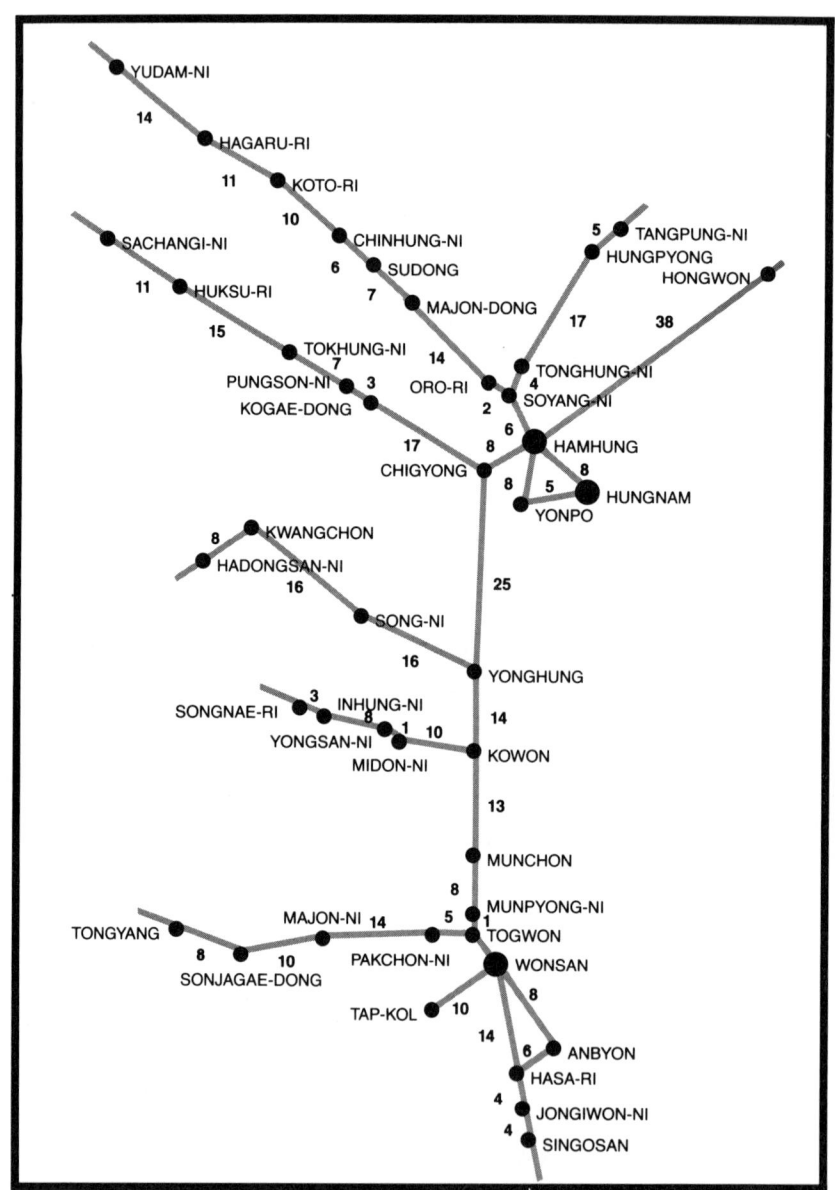

MAP No. 3 - Road Distances in Northeast Korea (in miles) - 1950

foot pass, that the 3d Infantry Division would fight its first engagement in Korea.

Moving north from Wonsan, along the road referred to as the MSR (main supply route) for units in X Corps, one passed through the village of Kowon and the town of Yonghung (twenty-six and thirty-six miles, respectively, from Wonsan) before entering Chigyong. This village, only eight miles southwest of Hamhung, was the site of another important road junction; one road led in a northwesterly direction to Huksu-ri, a distance of approximately forty-four miles, and to Sachang-ni, another eleven miles farther up the road.

The coastal plain of the Songchon estuary was one of the few level or semi-level areas, consisting of isolated pockets extending inland from the sea generally for a distance of three to five miles.

Situated on the northeast bank of the Songchon, where that river flowed into the sea, is Hungnam. This city contained a major port facility and also offered open beaches with a gradient favorable to amphibious operations if such became a necessity. The village of Yonpo with its modern airfield is located five miles away on the southwest bank of the river. Eight miles upstream from Hungnam is the city of Hamhung.[2]

Hamhung was a manufacturing center before the war and was also the site of a major road junction. The best road led in a northeasterly direction to Hongwon, a town farther up on the east coast. The more primitive road led due north to Soyang-ni. There one fork led northeasterly to Tonghung-ni, the other slanted northwest into the mountainous heart of North Korea toward the

Changjin (Chosin) Reservoir. It was along this road that the 1st Marine Division would soon be forced to fight its way to safety.

At the village of Oro-ri, eight miles north of Hamhung, the northern Taebaek range begins its rise from foothills to steep slopes and narrow twisting valleys. To one observer it most closely resembled the southern part of West Virginia around Logan, Mingo and McDowell counties but was even much sharper and more clearly defined than the Blue Ridge.[3]

Vegetation was sparse, with a few scrub trees in evidence. The road was little more than a well-rutted path of hard-packed dirt and gravel. It was wide enough for two-way traffic only as far as Chinhung-ni. Like the road from Wonsan to Hamhung, it included many hairpin turns that required trucks and tanks to stop and back up in order to pivot tightly enough to make a turn. The quarter-ton Jeep was the only vehicle capable of negotiating turns without the stop-and-back-up procedure, and even it could proceed only at speeds less than five miles per hour. Since much of the route was merely a ledge carved out of a mountainside, the opposite side of the road was generally a precipice dropping off for a thousand feet or more.[4]

Except for the 65th RCT, all elements of the 3d Infantry Division landed at Wonsan between November 11 and 20.[5] Upon arrival it was assigned to X Corps, commanded by Major General Edward M. Almond. The corps comprised the 1st Marine Division, 7th Infantry Division and several attached ROK units including the 26th ROK Regiment and the 1st and 3d ROK Marine Corps battalions.

Tactical military doctrine dictated the assignment of as many as three corps to a field army, a standard uniformly observed in Europe during World War II. Since EUSAK (Eighth United States Army in Korea) had but two corps at the time (I and IX corps), it was widely assumed that after the completion of the Inchon campaign, X Corps would pass from separate command to Eighth Army control. For reasons known only to himself and never fully explained, General MacArthur elected to continue the status quo with X Corps reporting directly to FECOM (Far East Command) headquarters in Tokyo.[6]

There were a number of anomalies in this decision. First, General Almond, the corps commander, continued to function as FECOM chief of staff, at least on paper. Second, logistical and supply problems inevitably cropped up when X Corps attempted to maintain stock levels that caused shortages in Eighth Army supplies. What may have started out as a healthy rivalry soon turned into animosity. Almost every aspect of the early days of the Korean conflict was characterized by make-do arrangements reflecting our nation's unpreparedness for war. It soon became evident, however, that one of the most serious problems facing the units assigned to X Corps would be the personality of the corps commander.[7]

Notes

1. Wonsan's 1950 population was estimated at 90,000.
2. Hamhung's 1950 population was estimated at 80,000.
3. Author interview: BG Harley F. Mooney, USA (Ret.), July 26, 1989.
4. For a comprehensive description of the terrain in northeast Korea, see Appleman, *South to the Naktong, North to the Yalu*, pp. 1–2, 685, 741–42; also Appleman, *East of Chosin*, pp. 12–14.
5. The 65th RCT (Regimental Combat Team) consisted of the 65th Infantry and attached artillery. This unit, whose assignment to the 3d Infantry Division is explained in chapter 2, had been in Korea since September 23, having sailed directly from Puerto Rico. Given the length of time these troops had trained together, they were judged to be prepared for a combat assignment earlier than the remainder of the division. Following several combat missions in September and October, the RCT was loaded aboard ship at Pusan and arrived at Wonsan on November 5–6, there to await the arrival of the 3d Infantry Division.
6. For an analysis of this controversial decision, see Martin Blemenson's "MacArthur's Divided Command" in the November 1956 issue of *Army* magazine.
7. The situation involving General Almond and his division commanders manifested itself early on. However, in order to avoid a disruption in the flow of the narrative, detailed consideration of the problem is deferred to the final chapter.

2

 War on a Shoestring

The Korean War began on Sunday, June 25, 1950, when North Korean troops poured across the 38th parallel, then the dividing line between the communist-dominated North Korean People's Republic and the Republic of Korea (South Korea).

South Korea's capital of Seoul fell within days, and it soon became evident the ROK (Republic of Korea) army was no match for the Soviet trained-and-equipped troops from the north. President Truman's decision to commit American ground forces (air and naval units were ordered in on June 27) was meant to bring order out of the chaos of defeat and to stiffen the spine of the ROK Army troops then in headlong retreat. American troops could do little to stem the tide as the North Koreans, led by large numbers of Russian-made T–34 tanks, swept everything before them.

As the North Koreans moved inexorably toward Pusan, it became obvious that the units from Japan, committed piecemeal with poorly conditioned troops and outmoded equipment, could only buy time for General Walton H. Walker's Eighth Army to organize defensive positions. Militarily, the situation in Korea looked bleak.

At Fort Lewis, Washington, the 2d Infantry Division was alerted for movement to the Far East, the first of many calls on the army's general reserve. At Fort Benning, Georgia, as well as at many other army posts, concern and frustration were very much in evidence during the first two weeks of July. Company-grade officers qualified as infantry platoon leaders were selected for immediate shipment to Korea, as were specialists in armor and artillery. As understrength units were committed to the fighting and combat losses mounted, entire battalions of infantry and artillery were rushed directly into the fray.[1]

By August 1 the situation was critical. One week later General Douglas MacArthur requested movement of the 82d Airborne Division to Korea. Since Russian aggression in Europe could not be ruled out, military leaders in Washington were reluctant to release the only combat-ready unit left in the general reserve. Accordingly, General MacArthur's request was denied.

Three days later a compromise was struck that was generally acceptable to all concerned. The depleted state of the 3d Infantry Division at Fort Benning placed a limit on its value as a combat-ready unit. Army planners in Washington recommended replacing the 30th Infantry Regiment, then at zero strength, with the 65th Infantry Regiment based in Puerto Rico.[2] The 64th Heavy Tank Battalion and the 58th Armored Field Artillery Battalion, then part of the 2d Armored Division at Fort Hood, Texas, would be replacement units for the 73d Heavy Tank Battalion and the 9th and 41st Field Artillery battalions sent to Korea in the July personnel levies.

By a rationale that can only be described as sheer desperation, Army Field Forces headquarters estimated that the reconstituted 3d Division would be at 40 percent combat effectiveness once these new units had been assimilated. It authorized the movement of the division to Japan with the understanding that General MacArthur would agree to its being given a training period of sixty days in order to fill its ranks, draw necessary equipment, and achieve a basic level of proficiency and cohesion before being committed to combat in Korea.

From an historical perspective, it is important to note that the amphibious landing at Inchon had not taken place at the time the 3d Infantry Division departed the United States. Military leaders in Washington were aware that this operation, though a high-risk venture, had the potential to end the war. In that event, plans called for most of Eighth Army to return to Japan, with the 2d Infantry and 3d Infantry Divisions going directly to Europe. If occupation forces were required in Korea, the unit most likely to remain behind was the 3d Infantry Division, under the direction of X Corps.[3]

As General Walker's Eighth Army fought on gallantly, plans were being made to turn the tide. A flanking operation deep in the enemy's rear was one means of relieving enemy pressure along the Naktong River line. Such a movement was conceived and ordered into planning by General MacArthur over the skepticism of staff members in Tokyo and Washington. This operation ranks among his greatest exploits.

The amphibious assault at Inchon on September 15 took the North Koreans by surprise. Suddenly faced with the prospect of having their supply lines severed, the communist forces far to the south had no choice but to react to what was happening in their rear.

Spearheaded by the 1st Marine Division (now up to full wartime strength) and supported by elements of the 7th Infantry Division (its own personnel shortages having been offset by a contingent of Korean nationals pressed into military service), the newly activated X Corps quickly advanced to liberate the capital at Seoul and seal off all avenues of escape.

Military victory was no longer in doubt. The next decision, a political one, was whether to stop the United Nations forces at the 38th parallel or to reunite the two Koreas forcibly under the terms of post World War II agreements between Russia and the Western Allies.

On October 7 the United Nations Security Council approved a resolution authorizing U.N. ground forces to move into North Korean territory. By October 19 elements of the ROK 1st and 7th divisions occupied the North Korean capital of Pyongyang.

Meanwhile, the 1st Marine and 7th Infantry Divisions, the Inchon assault force, were alerted for another amphibious operation. The marine division was outloaded from Inchon while the 7th Infantry Division moved by motor transport to Pusan. Still assigned to X Corps, they were given the mission of landing at the North Korean port city of Wonsan. Unfortunately, Wonsan harbor was heavily mined, and on October 9, before the minefield could be cleared, the ROK 3d and Capital divisions entered the city.

On October 15 a meeting of historic importance took place on Wake Island. In the only face to face meeting between them, President Truman traveled halfway around the world to meet his field commander and to assess the situation in Korea. One of his first questions to General MacArthur was to solicit the general's opinion on the chances of intervention in Korea by the Chinese Communists. MacArthur replied: "Very little. Had they interfered in the first or second months, it would have been decisive. We are no longer fearful of their intervention. We no longer stand hat in hand."[4]

For one of the few times in his life, Douglas MacArthur was wrong. It was an error that would cost many lives.

Notes

1. The critical personnel shortages in combat units can best be understood by examining a partial list of the frenetic shuffling of infantry regiments and battalions that took place July 4–August 10, 1950:

a) 5th Regimental Combat Team in Hawaii: Sent to Korea and attached to 25th Inf Div. Eventually replaced 34th Inf (24th Inf Div) when that unit was disbanded.
b) 29th Infantry on Okinawa: 1/29th Inf became 3/35th Inf (25th Inf Div); 3/29th Inf became 3/27th Inf (25th Inf Div).
c) 14th Infantry at Fort Carson, CO: 3/14th Inf became 3/5th Cav (1st Cav Div).

d) 7th Infantry at Fort Devens, MA: 3/7th Inf became 3/8th Cav (1st Cav Div).

e) 30th Infantry at Fort Benning, GA: 2/30th Inf became 3/7th Cav (1st Cav Div); 30th Infantry placed on inactive status.

f) 33d Infantry in Panama: 3/33d Inf became 3/65th Inf (3d Inf Div).

g) 65th Infantry in Puerto Rico: Replaced 30th Inf in 3d Inf Div. This cannibalization resulted in the commitment to combat of units and newly assigned commanders without the benefit of having trained or worked together, a situation to be avoided if at all possible.

2. Organized shortly after the end of the Spanish-American War (1898), the 65th Infantry was primarily composed of residents of Puerto Rico and the Virgin Islands. It was a source of ethnic pride for the islanders to serve in their own regiment.

Because the U. S. Army was still segregated in 1950, the 65th Infantry was regarded as a "colored" unit, thereby limiting opportunities for its members to be assigned to other units.

As a result, the regiment enjoyed a higher-than-average level of experience among its senior noncommissioned officers who are the backbone of any military unit. However, the 65th Infantry, as indicated in Note 1 above, did share with other infantry regiments the handicap of being at 60–70 percent of its authorized strength.

3. See James F. Schnabel, *U.S. Army in Korea—Policy and Direction: The First Year*, pp. 132–34, 222–24, quoting radiograms Rad JCS 94651, JCS to CINCFE, 21 October 1950; Rad C 677985, Bolte (Personal) for Collins; and Rad JCS 95625, JCS to CINCFE, 3 November 1950.

4. "Substance of Statements Made at Wake Island." A stenographic transcript prepared by Ms. Vernice Anderson at Wake Island on October 15, 1950, and submitted by the Joint Chiefs of Staff to committees of the U.S. Senate.

3

 Prelude to Combat

The USS *General William A. Mann* (AP-112) slipped her moorings at San Francisco's Fort Mason pier shortly before noon on August 30, 1950, and headed out into the long swells of the Pacific Ocean. She was followed shortly by four sister ships as they carried the understrength 3d Infantry Division to Japan.[1]

Upon its arrival on September 12, the division was transported to Camp Chickamauga near Beppu on the island of Kyushu. Individual and unit training began at once.

The new division commander, Major General Robert H. Soule, was an excellent choice for a unit new to combat and new to the Orient. Soule was born in Laramie, Wyoming, on February 10, 1900. He attended the University of Wyoming for two years and was commissioned a second lieutenant in the Infantry Reserve on September 16, 1918. Following brief assignments at Camp Hancock, Georgia, and Camp Lewis, Washington, he served with the 31st Infantry as part of the Allied Expeditionary Force which opposed the Bolshevik (Red) Army in Siberia. He returned with the 31st Infantry to its duty station at Fort McKinley, Philippine Islands, in April 1920, three months prior to receiving his regular army commission.

Lieutenant Soule was assigned to the 38th Infantry at Fort Douglas, Utah, for a period of five years that began in July 1922. In September 1927 he entered The Infantry School, Fort Benning, Georgia, and upon graduation one year later he joined the 29th Infantry.

Soule went to Peking, China, in October 1929 as a language student. In May 1933 he assumed command of a rifle company, and subsequently of a battalion of the 7th Infantry at Vancouver Barracks, Washington. He returned to Tientsin, China, in March 1937, where he served with the 15th Infantry as company commander and regimental intelligence officer. He was rated as fluent in Russian and in several Chinese dialects.

He entered the Command and General Staff School at Fort Leavenworth, Kansas, in September 1939 and upon graduation in February 1940 was assigned to the 16th Infantry at Fort Benning, Georgia. His combat experience in World War II included command of the 188th Glider Infantry, 11th Airborne Division. He commanded the regiment through the Leyte campaign, participated in the liberation of Manila and was promoted to brigadier general on March 20, 1945. In the aftermath of World War II, Soule was assigned to Chunking as assistant military attache. With the demise of the Nationalist government on mainland China in the autumn of 1949, he was under virtual house arrest for almost six months until he could return to the United States.

He was promoted to major general in August 1950 and placed in command of the 3d Infantry Division, then in the final stages of preparation for its departure to Japan.

General Soule spared neither his staff nor himself in whipping the division into shape for deployment in Korea. He seemed to be everywhere at once, as likely to step out of a light aircraft as a jeep in visiting the various units as they conducted their training programs. When deficiencies were noted, he expected prompt corrective action.

As one young officer remembered him years later, General Soule "had a remarkable impact on me and most of my contemporaries. We believed in him."[2] Greatly respected by General Ridgway, General Soule commanded the division until October 1951, the first (army) division commander to complete a full year's tour in Korea.[3]

Brigadier General Armistead D. Mead (USMA '24) was the assistant division commander. At forty-nine years of age, he had been a senior staff officer in the European theatre in World War II.[4]

Fifty-one-year-old Colonel Oliver P. Newman (USMA '22), the chief of staff, commanded a regiment in the Pacific and rose to chief of staff of the 41st Infantry Division before Japan surrendered.

Division Artillery (referred to as "DivArty") was under the command of fifty-seven-year-old Brigadier General Roland P. Shugg (USMA '16).

The division general staff was composed of:

G–1 Major (later LTC) James W. Friend
G–2 LTC Ned B. Broyles (USMA '36)
G–3 LTC Nathaniel R. Hoskot
G–4 LTC Erwin O. Gibson

The division special staff included:

Div Engineer	LTC Leslie M. Gross
Div Signal Officer	LTC Robert R. Malone
Div Quartermaster	LTC Stanley H. Partridge
Div Chemical Officer	LTC James E. Rogers
Div Surgeon	LTC Joseph K. Bayne
Div Finance Officer	LTC Olin T. Hinkley
Adjutant General	LTC Robert E. Doe
Inspector General	LTC Julius Levy
Provost Marshal	LTC Clifford B. Hill
Staff Judge Advocate	LTC Nathaniel B. Rieger
Division Chaplain	LTC (Father) Peter S. Rush

Captain John T. Daniel and 1st Lieutenant Jack Tomlinson served as aides to General Soule, while 1st Lieutenant Harley F. Mooney served as aide to General Mead. Lieutenant Mooney would later distinguish himself in combat in both Korea and Vietnam before retiring as a brigadier general.

The real "heavyweight," however, was the deputy chief of staff, thirty-four-year-old Lieutenant Colonel Fred C. Weyand, a University of California ROTC graduate who would shine as a battalion commander in the 7th Infantry, later serve two tours in Vietnam (the last one as commander-in-chief of all American ground forces) and conclude his military career as the army's chief of staff (1974–76).

The 7th Infantry was commanded by Colonel John S. Guthrie (USMA '30), then forty-two years of age. His executive officer, forty-year-old LTC James O. Boswell (USMA '33), would prove an excellent replacement when Colonel Guthrie moved up to X Corps early in 1951 as chief of staff to Major General Almond.

Battalion commanders in the 7th Infantry were:

1st LTC Charles T. Heinrich
2d LTC Robert Besson (USMA '37)
3d LTC Thomas A. O'Neill (USMA '34)

LTC Weyand moved from division staff early in 1951 to replace LTC Heinrich. Major (later LTC) Samuel G. Kail (USMA '39) replaced LTC Besson on December 5, 1950. Besson was injured when his jeep was accidentally strafed by a U.S. Navy jet. Major George Mitchell, 3d Bn X/O, would prove his worth as a combat leader in his performance with Task Force Dog, the ad hoc command formed for the purpose of fighting its way northward to Chinhung-ni to hold open the escape route for the beleaguered marine division.

The 10th Field Artillery Battalion, supporting the 7th Infantry was commanded by forty-three-year-old LTC Walter A. Downing (USMA '33).

The 15th Infantry was commanded by Colonel Dennis M. Moore (USMA '24). The fifty-year-old Moore had been captured by the Japanese in the Philippines in 1942. His three years as a prisoner of war had aged him considerably beyond his years, and he was neither physically nor mentally prepared for another tour of combat duty.[5]

Forty-two-year-old LTC Thomas R. Yancey was executive officer under Colonel Moore and had extensive experience in amphibious warfare in the Pacific.

Battalion commanders in the 15th Infantry were:

1st LTC Robert M. Blanchard (USMA '33)
2d LTC Allen L. Peck (USMA '36)
3d LTC Edward L. Farrell, Jr.
LTC Farrell replaced LTC Milburn N. Huston shortly after arrival in Korea.

The 39th Field Artillery Battalion, firing in support of the 15th Infantry, was commanded by forty-two-year-old LTC Robert B. Neely (USMA '33).

The 65th Infantry, which replaced the depleted 30th Infantry and had sailed directly from Puerto Rico to Korea, was commanded by Colonel William W. Harris (USMA '30), then forty-three years old. His executive officer was thirty-nine-year-old LTC George W. Childs (USMA '36).

Battalion commanders in the 65th Infantry were:

1st LTC Howard B. St. Clair (USMA '39)
2d LTC Herman W. Dammer
3d Major E. G. Allen
Major Allen's battalion had been part of the 33d Infantry Regiment in Panama prior to the movement to Korea.

It is significant to note that all three infantry regiments in the 3d Infantry Division had one "reconstituted" battalion.

The 58th Armored Field Artillery, commanded by thirty-three-year-old LTC Harry A. Stella (USMA '40) fired in support of the 65th Infantry.

The 999th Armored Field Artillery Battalion, equipped with eighteen 155mm self-propelled howitzers mounted on M–26 tank chassis, was

M–46 tanks from the 3d Infantry Division's 64th Heavy Tank Battalion in hull defilade position at Kogae-dong near Hamhung. These tanks were withdrawn from the beachhead a few days before the final evacuation since their gun tubes could not be sufficiently elevated to provide short range, high angle fire as the Chinese forces moved closer to the beachhead. U.S. Army Photo 111–SC–354096, courtesy of National Archives.

A 155mm howitzer in action on the Hungnam perimeter. These self-propelled units of the 3d Infantry Division's 999th Armored Field Artillery Battalion were capable of delivering high angle fire at a rapid rate. U.S. Army Photo 111-SC-354865, courtesy of National Archives.

Russian SU–76 self-propelled guns, captured from the North Koreans, were among the thousands of vehicles outloaded by the Navy at Hungnam during the final days of the evacuation in December 1950. U.S. Army Photo 111-SC-355022, courtesy of National Archives.

Hundreds of tanks, trucks, jeeps and other vehicles await loading aboard ships in mid-December 1950 during the withdrawal at Hungnam in North Korea. U.S. Army Photo 111-SC-355086, courtesy of National Archives.

An Army M-19 self-propelled gun carriage, mounting twin 40mm Bofors guns, is shown being loaded aboard a Navy transport at Hungnam in December 1950. U.S. Army Photo 111-SC-354883, courtesy of National Archives.

A "before and after" series of photos showing the destruction of a railroad viaduct in North Korea as the withdrawal of the United Nations forces began in December 1950. U.S. Army Photos 111–SC–355246 and 111–SC–355247, courtesy of National Archives.

Soldiers of the 3d Infantry Division boarding the USNS *General H. B. Freeman* (AP–143) on December 24, 1950. The U.S. Navy played a prominent role in the successful evacuation of the Hungnam beachhead. U.S. Army Photo 111-SC-355420, courtesy of National Archives.

Troops of the 7th Infantry Regiment, 3d Infantry Division, wade out to waiting landing craft on December 24, 1950, in the final hours of the Hungnam evacuation. U.S. Army Photo 111–SC–355588, courtesy of National Archives.

commanded by thirty-nine-year-old LTC Kenneth F. Dawalt (USMA '36).

Rounding out the artillery component of the division was the 3d AAA (AW) Battalion commanded by LTC Alvin Newbury.[6] This battalion's mission was to provide anti-aircraft protection with its four firing batteries. It was equipped with a total of thirty-two M–16s and M–19s.

The M–16 was a half-tracked vehicle (conventional wheels on the front axle, a tracked suspension on the rear) and equipped with four .50 caliber machine guns. These guns could be fired as a unit or singly.

The M–19 was mounted on a fully tracked M–24 tank chassis and equipped with twin-mounted 40mm Bofors guns that fired in tandem.

The enemy in Korea possessed no tactical air arm to speak of. Nevertheless, the 3d AAA AW Battalion, with its rapid-fire capability, provided the infantry with an effective means of fighting off the huge numbers of enemy troops who seemed quite willing to die. The enemy's resolve was noticeably tempered by these automatic weapons.

As noted previously, the 64th Heavy Tank Battalion was newly joined from 2d Armored Division at Fort Hood. This fine unit was equipped with the newer M–46 tank (90mm gun) and was commanded by LTC William G. Bartlett, Jr. (USMA '33).

On August 6, 1950, prior to its departure from Fort Benning, the 3rd Infantry Division's strength was a mere 5,179 (18,894 authorized).

As late as September 30 it was a rare instance in which any rifle squad in the 7th and 15th infantry regiments had more than four men per squad. On that date, the company strengths in the 7th Infantry were:

	Authorized Strength			Actual Strength		
	Officers	Warrant Officers	Enlisted Men	Officers	Warrant Officers	Enlisted Men
Co A	06	00	205	06	01	036
Co B	06	00	205	06	00	046
Co C	06	00	205	06	01	036
Co D	05	00	160	05	01	043
Co E	06	00	205	06	01	037
Co F	06	00	205	06	01	037
Co G	06	00	205	06	01	036
Co H	05	00	160	05	01	027
Co I	06	00	205	06	01	034
Co K	06	00	205	05	01	032
Co L	06	00	205	05	01	037
Co M	05	00	160	05	01	037

Figures for comparable units in the 15th Infantry were somewhat higher but still far below the 205 men called for in the T/O&E.

Having left the United States at roughly 40 percent of its authorized strength, the division had to await the arrival of 1,500 fillers just completing basic or refresher training in the U.S.

Also, approximately 8,500 Korean nationals en route to Japan for training would be assigned to the 3d Division.

A number of problems arose with the KATUSAs (Korean Augmentation to the United States Army). The obvious language barrier to communication was resolved to a workable degree, according to 1st

Lt (later Lieutenant General) Pat Crizer in 3/7th Infantry by "sign language and a lot of four-letter words." This was soon surpassed by feeding (standard army field rations made no provision for the Oriental dietary staple of unpolished rice) and safety (when live ammunition was issued for training purposes). The lack of sanitation training and the Koreans' tendency to let nature take its course wherever they happened to be standing or sitting, was much harder to cope with.[7]

Most KATUSAs subsequently proved to be unreliable in combat, especially in the role of infantrymen, and as additional American fillers became available in the replacement pipeline, every unit in the division made a supreme effort to obtain its share as quickly as possible.[8] However, the Koreans retained by the division as translators proved invaluable in the dark days of December, since many were natives of northeast Korea, where the fighting took place. They also helped overcome the Caucasian inability to distinguish North Koreans from Chinese.

The lack of personnel continued to hamper the division even after its arrival in Korea. On November 23 more than half of the infantry battalions were still short of personnel:

2/15th Infantry—69.68% of authorized strength
1/15th Infantry—72.73% of authorized strength
2/ 7th Infantry—74.15% of authorized strength
1/ 7th Infantry—74.59% of authorized strength
3/ 7th Infantry—76.33% of authorized strength
2/65th Infantry—98.80% of authorized strength

1/65th Infantry—101.63% of authorized strength
3/15th Infantry—102.18% of authorized strength
3/65th Infantry—103.00% of authorized strength

Given that its organizational and training cycle were severely curtailed, the wonder is that this or any army unit sent to Korea was able to function effectively in combat. The first crisis faced in Korea, however, was the state of the division's signal equipment.

Notes

1. USS *General A. W. Brewster* (AP–155); USS *General William O. Darby* (AP–127); USS *General Hugh J. Gaffey* (AP–121); USS *General Daniel I. Sultan* (AP–120)

2. Author interview, BG Harley F. Mooney, USA (Ret.), July 26, 1989.

3. Upon his return to the United States, General Soule was assigned to Fort Monroe, VA, as inspector of infantry. He died of a heart attack in Washington, DC, on January 19, 1952, three months after leaving Korea and three weeks short of his fifty-second birthday.

4. Information in this chapter on West Point graduates was obtained from "Register of Graduates, United States Military Academy," 1988 edition. Unfortunately, the author was unable to verify the source of commissioning for officers who were not West Point graduates. While some few may have received direct or "battlefield" commissions or appointment in the National Guard, it is believed that most were commissioned through the R.O.T.C. program or Officer Candidate School.

5. Mooney, interview.

6. A relatively new addition to the infantry division, the AAA AW (Automatic Weapons) battalion was added just prior to the United States' entry into World War II, when the Ger-

man Army, in its lightning war in France, demonstrated the havoc that close air support could wreak on ground troops.

7. Author interview, LTG Pat W. Crizer, USA (Ret.), June 3, 1989.

8. Command Report—7th Infantry Regiment, December 1950.

4
Problems in Communications

In today's noisy world of miniaturized transistor radios, it is difficult to realize that just forty years ago radio communication was nowhere as reliable as it is today.

At the time the Korean war began, FM (frequency modulation) was in its infancy. AM (amplitude modulation) was the primary system available, and there were severe limitations to its use in combat.

The field radios were bulky. Their effective range was hampered by land masses such as mountains and by atmospheric conditions. In the subzero temperatures of that first Korean winter, they consumed batteries at an alarming rate.

Although there were several types of AM radios in the hands of the troops—primarily World War II vintage and not in mint condition—the Korean War was primarily a "wire" war.

Through the use of field telephones and switchboards, infantry rifle and heavy weapons companies could communicate with their own internal elements and adjacent units as well as with their battalion headquarters. Army signal procedure dictated that communications support be provided by the higher headquarters to the lower headquarters and (facing the enemy) from the unit on the left to the unit on the right.[1]

In the early stages of the war, wire between regimental and battalion headquarters was rare—thus, radio became the only dependable link to command posts at battalion level and above.[2] Artillery battalions maintained wire communications when in direct support of infantry regiments.

Most of the wire was laid on the ground; burying wire was rare since such work was time-consuming. Yet lines on the ground had the obvious handicap of being susceptible to breaks caused by friendly as well as enemy forces. Trucks and tracked vehicles were the worst hazards, but mortar and artillery fire also caused considerable damage. To overcome obstacles such as rivers, stream beds and blown bridges, the use of poles and trees was often necessary.

This communications network frequently required the use of as much as 150 miles of wire in a regimental sector in the course of combat operations.

Radio equipment included the hand-held "walkie-talkie" (SCR 536), an AM radio with a single, preset crystal channel and a maximum range of one mile under optimum conditions. This was the primary radio link between an infantry company commander and his platoons on the line until it was replaced by the AN/PRC 6, an FM radio with superior operating range, reliability, and more frequencies.

For communicating with battalion headquarters, the company commander had two FM radios (SCR 300), both on the battalion net and with a maximum of 170 channels. These radios had a practical range of three to eight miles, again subject to constraints of terrain and weather.

At battalion level an AM radio (AN/GRC 9, called the "Angry 9") was the primary radio link to the regiment. Artillery units firing in direct support of the infantry furnished artillery liaison officers and forward observers who were equipped with the SCR 619 (FM) and the AN/PRC 9 with 120 channels. Since armored units were equipped with the 80-channel (FM) AN/PRC 8, an exchange of operators with the infantry was frequently required for effective communications, inasmuch as the AN/PRC 8, AN/PRC 9 and AN/PRC 10 were on different frequencies. This situation can best be visualized by referring to Table 2.[3]

At regimental level the AN/GRC 9 was also used for communicating with subordinate units, sister units, and division headquarters. A detachment from divisional level, equipped with a vehicle-mounted and more powerful AM radio (SCR 193), was frequently attached to regimental headquarters to assure radio contact with division headquarters when distances were too great for the AN/GRC 9.

Not only did the personnel requisitions of July 1950 strip the regiments of their best communications personnel, but the equipment in the hands of the troops was, for the most part, in poor condition. 1st Lieutenant (later Major) Joseph J. Piaseczny, the communications officer for 1st Battalion, 7th Infantry and eventually regimental communications officer, had seen enough combat in World War II to appreciate the necessity for

Table 2

FREQUENCY OVERLAPS IN MEGACYCLES—FM RADIOS

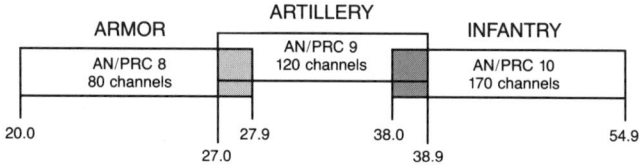

There were 350 channels available on the Armor-Artillery-Infantry net, with a 100 kilocycle separation between channels. The field artillery, by virtue of having its 120 channels on a spectrum running from 27.0 Mc to 38.9 Mc, had a small overlap with armor and infantry units. This allowed the artillery, when providing fire support, to enter the armor or infantry net without exchanging equipment.

Infantry and armor units usually exchanged equipment with the former providing [the] equipment and operator to the latter. In emergency situations, the artillery overlap also provided an alternate means of communication between infantry and armor.

Source: Major Joseph J. Piaseczny, U.S. Army (Ret.)

scrounging any extra radio equipment that might come his way. Shortly before departing Fort Devens in August 1950, he was able to obtain new equipment without having to surrender the worn-out radios then being replaced. His ability to improvise and use the old radios for spare parts gave his unit an advantage over many battalions then heading for combat.[4]

An organizational chart will reflect who is in

nominal charge of a military unit; however, it is men like Joe Piaseczny that really make things work.

Notes

1. The author is indebted to MAJ Joseph J. Piaseczny, USA (Ret.), for providing the technical information in this chapter.

2. As the fighting entered its second year and stabilized into positional warfare, telephone communications between regimental headquarters and the front line battalions was greatly improved with the establishment of a regimental switching center roughly three miles behind the front line. Its location was left to the discretion of the regimental communications officer.

3. This problem was not solved until 1965, well after the cessation of fighting in Korea, with the introduction of the AN/PRC 25, a 980 channel FM radio that made such exchanges unnecessary

4. Piaseczny interview.

5

 GUERRILLA WARFARE

When the 3d Infantry Division went ashore in northeast Korea, its initial mission was to relieve the 1st Marine Division of responsibility for defending an area that exceeded three thousand square miles.[1] This was an unrealistically large area for an infantry division to control or defend, because the divisional units were to be widely separated. Since the combat phase of operations appeared to be winding down after the successful landing at Inchon, General Almond, X Corps commander, considered it to be a gamble worth taking even though the terrain militated against it.

X Corps Order No. 6, issued November 11, returned the 65th Infantry to division control, attached certain ROK units (3d and 5th ROK Marine battalions, 26th ROK Infantry Regiment) to the division and directed preparation for offensive operations to the west, toward the Eighth Army sector. It also directed the division to station one infantry battalion in Hamhung as corps reserve. 3d Division Operations Order No. 1 refined this mission by establishing regimental combat teams. The 7th Infantry (minus one battalion in corps reserve) would provide the nucleus for the 7th RCT, with the attachment of the 10th Field Artillery Battalion; Battery A, 3d AAA AW Battalion; Company A, 10th Engineer (C) Battalion, plus detachments from the 3d Medical Battalion and 3d Signal Company. This RCT and the 64th Heavy Tank Battalion (minus Companies B and C) constituted the division reserve and was given the mission of securing the coastal area from Togwon (a village just north of Wonsan) to Hungnam, and of safeguarding railroad bridges and construction sites. On November 17, the RCT established its command post (CP) at Kowon, a village situated on the Main Supply Route (MSR).

The 15th Infantry formed the nucleus for the 15th RCT with the attachment of the 39th Field Artillery Battalion; the remainder of the 3d AAA AW Battalion; Company B, 64th Heavy Tank Battalion; Company B, 10th Engineer (C) Battalion, plus detachments from the 3d Medical Battalion and 3d Signal Company. The 3d KMC (Korean Marine Corps) Battalion and the 5th KMC Battalion (minus 23d Company) were also assigned to the RCT.

This RCT was assigned responsibility for securing Wonsan and the area south and west of the town, with the main effort to be made westward along the Wonsan-Majon-ni axis. On November 12 it established its CP at Togwon, three miles north and west of Wonsan.

The 65th Infantry was the basic unit for the 65th RCT with the attachment of the 58th Armored Field Artillery Battalion; Company C, 64th Heavy Tank Battalion; Company C, 10th Engineer (C) Battalion; and detachments from the 3d Medical Battalion and 3d Signal Company. It was directed to continue operations in the west central portion of the division sector with its main effort along the Yonghung-Hadongsan-ni axis (a distance of approximately forty miles). This made Yonghung, a village on the MSR and roughly midway between Wonsan and Hamhung, the logical location for its command post.

A fourth RCT was built around the 26th ROK Infantry Regiment with the attachment of Battery A, 96th Field Artillery Battalion, and a detachment from the 3d Signal Company. It was given responsibility for the northern part of the division sector west of Hamhung and the mission of patrolling westward to the Eighth Army-X Corps boundary. On November 11 this RCT established its CP at Kogae-dong, a village about seventeen miles northwest of Chigyong and roughly fifteen to seventeen miles due west of Hamhung. These RCT assignments would remain basically unchanged until December 12 and the beginning of the Hungnam operation.

Bypassed bands of roving guerrillas, some of them five hundred strong, were making their way northward through the division zone of operations in an effort to reestablish contact with elements of the NKPA.

It soon became evident they would be much more difficult to control than was originally thought possible. Just how difficult became evident on November 12 when the 1/15th Infantry, commanded by LTC Robert M. Blanchard, attempted to move a column to Majon-ni in relief of a battalion of marines.

Blanchard's battalion had departed Wonsan at first light on the morning of November 12. About halfway to its destination, the battalion came upon a small stream where the bridge had been destroyed. A perimeter was established while a small attached engineer unit began repairing the bridge.

The repair operation consumed the remaining daylight hours, and at dusk, the American soldiers began firing their weapons at what they believed to be enemy troops. Realizing that nervousness among troops new to combat is a common occurrence, Colonel Blanchard, with little regard for his own safety, restored control by boldly walking down the road toward the bridge site and ordering his troops to cease firing.

Movement to Majon-ni was resumed the next morning and the marine battalion was relieved. 1/15th Infantry established its command post in an abandoned school building. Combat patrols were conducted during daylight hours and the battalion "buttoned up" in its perimeter area at dusk, since the enemy generally attacked at night.

Getting supplies to the 3d Korean Marine Corps Battalion at Tongyang, a village about eighteen miles farther west of Majon-ni, proved to be a problem. On November 21, 1/15th Infantry sent a motorized patrol of approximately one hundred men westward from Majon-ni to make contact with the Korean marine units. The NKPA guerrillas had established an ambush above a defile about midway between the two villages. Their position on a ridge about 150 feet above the roadway gave them complete command of the terrain. An air strike failed to dislodge the enemy, and American losses in men, weapons and vehicles were substantial.[2]

Success in breaking through the roadblock was finally achieved, after three attempts, on November 25. A coordinated attack, made from both directions (3d KMC Battalion moving east and 1/15th Infantry moving west), caught the enemy in between. The NKPA guerrillas suffered heavy casualties as well as the loss of several 120mm mortars and an arms cache near Sonjagae-dong, a village midway between Majon-ni and Tongyang.[3]

Patrols from the 3d Recon Company noted enemy activity south of Wonsan in the vicinity of Singosan. One patrol surprised a group of approximately one hundred guerrillas setting fires between Singosan and Jongiwon-ni. In the skirmish that followed, twenty-six enemy were killed and seven taken prisoner. Refugees fleeing Singosan reported an enemy force of one thousand men preparing for an attack on Anbyon, just thirteen miles south of Wonsan. (See Map 4.)

To counter this enemy thrust, 3d Recon Company and a naval gunfire team from the USS *Rochester* were sent to destroy the enemy forces in Singosan. The 5th KMC Battalion, reinforced with one platoon from Tank Company, 15th Infantry, and one battery from 39th Field Artillery was ordered to follow the Recon company as far as Anbyon. From this base the battalion was to conduct aggressive patrolling to the south, southeast, and west. Finding Anbyon deserted, the battalion continued south for another six miles to Hasa-ri where it attacked an enemy force and drove them off, taking twenty prisoners. Continuing the advance to Singosan, 5th KMC Battalion found that village to be heavily fortified; the battalion with-

3D INFANTRY DIV. SITUATION MAP
NOVEMBER 11 - 24, 1950

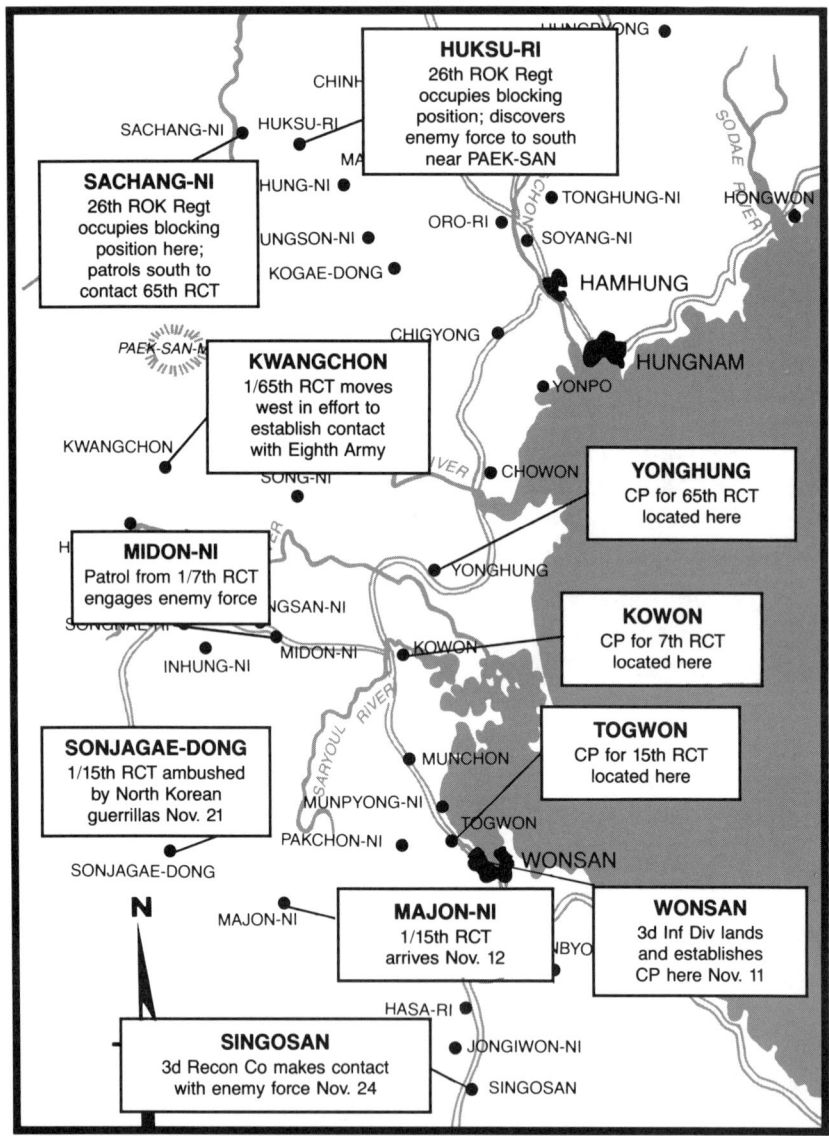

MAP No. 4

drew to Anbyon prior to darkness and requested an air strike for the following morning. Shortly after daylight on November 25 one company of Korean marines, supported by a section of tanks, returned to Singosan and found the enemy had withdrawn.

While the 15th Infantry was having its troubles south and west of Wonsan, Colonel Harris's 65th Infantry had not been idle. Situated in the center of the division sector, the 65th was poised to strike in a westerly direction which was still considered the 3d Division's main axis of operations.

LTC Howard B. St. Clair's 1/65th Infantry had been ordered to move west from Yonghung to the village of Kwangchon, a distance of twenty air miles, but thirty-two of the most tortuous road miles Colonel St. Clair ever traveled. Patrols from this battalion sought to make contact with a patrol from the Eighth Army for four consecutive days beginning on November 10.[4] On the last day 1/65th made contact with a patrol from 2d Battalion, 10th ROK Regiment, at a point believed to be several miles beyond the boundary line between X Corps and Eighth Army. This was the only physical contact made between the two U. N. commands in North Korea.[5]

In an attempt to establish contact with the 26th ROK Regiment and to reconnoiter a reported enemy buildup in the vicinity of Paek-san, Company B, 65th Infantry moved north to Paek-san on November 18. The company was not successful in establishing contact with the 26th ROK Regiment, but it did make contact with a strong enemy force. Company B took up a defensive position on high ground, where it succeeded in beating off an enemy force armed with mortars and automatic weapons. An airdrop replenished supplies of food and ammunition, and the attack was repulsed.

On November 18, 26th ROK Regiment was ordered to attack, seize and hold Huksu-ri, a village about fifty-two miles northwest of Hamhung, until relieved by elements of the 1st Marine Division. The following day the regiment moved to Tokhung (fifteen miles short of Huksu-ri) in preparation for the attack. Huksu-ri was taken on November 20 against light resistance.

On November 21 a patrol from 1/7th Infantry, attached to the 65th RCT, made a reconnaissance of the area west of Kowon. Ten miles west of Kowon, near the village of Midon-ni, an enemy force of company size was entrenched on both sides of the road. A firefight ensued, but the enemy force broke contact under cover of a brush fire started by tracer ammunition.

Logistical support for the 26th ROK Regiment posed problems due to the lack of roads in their sector. On November 21, X Corps agreed to a boundary change between 26th ROK and the 1st Marine Division in order to place the road from Huksu-ri to Sachang-ni within the 3d Division zone.

The 26th ROK Regiment was ordered to establish blocking positions at Sachang-ni and Huksu-ri; to patrol south to gain contact with the 65th RCT; to patrol north to contact the 1st Marine Division; and patrol west to establish contact with the Eighth Army. Shortly after establishing these blocking positions, the regiment found all three of its battalions under enemy attack. Enemy pressure was strongest at Sachang-ni and it appeared this regiment was in danger of being overwhelmed. Therefore, 7th Infantry was ordered to move its 2d and 3d battalions (1st Battalion was still attached to 65th RCT) by rail and motor march to Hamhung for the purpose of relieving or reinforcing the 26th ROK. However, upon arrival at Hamhung, 7th RCT was ordered into corps reserve.

Enemy activity, which had been sporadic, suddenly erupted everywhere. As the tempo increased (and rumors of Chinese prisoners became widespread), 7th Infantry was released from corps reserve to division control with the mission of relieving the 26th ROK Regiment which, in turn, would pass from 3d Division to X Corps control.

On November 25, 1/7th Infantry relieved 26th ROK at Sachang-ni; 2d and 3d battalions moved the next day to the vicinity of Kogae-dong (thirty-eight miles east of Sachang-ni).

Around 7:30 P.M. on November 27 enemy forces began an artillery barrage that struck the positions of 1/7th Infantry at Sachang-ni. Two hours later a full-scale attack by an estimated eight hundred enemy troops was under way. The battalion CP and fire direction center were knocked out and communications with the rifle companies was disrupted. This attack (confirmed later as a reconnaissance in force by the CCF units at Yudam-ni probing for an open flank) continued into the next day, and was repelled at daybreak. Small-arms fire continued throughout the day and the Charlie Company positions, which had been breached, were restored.

3D INFANTRY DIV. SITUATION MAP

NOVEMBER 25 - 30, 1950

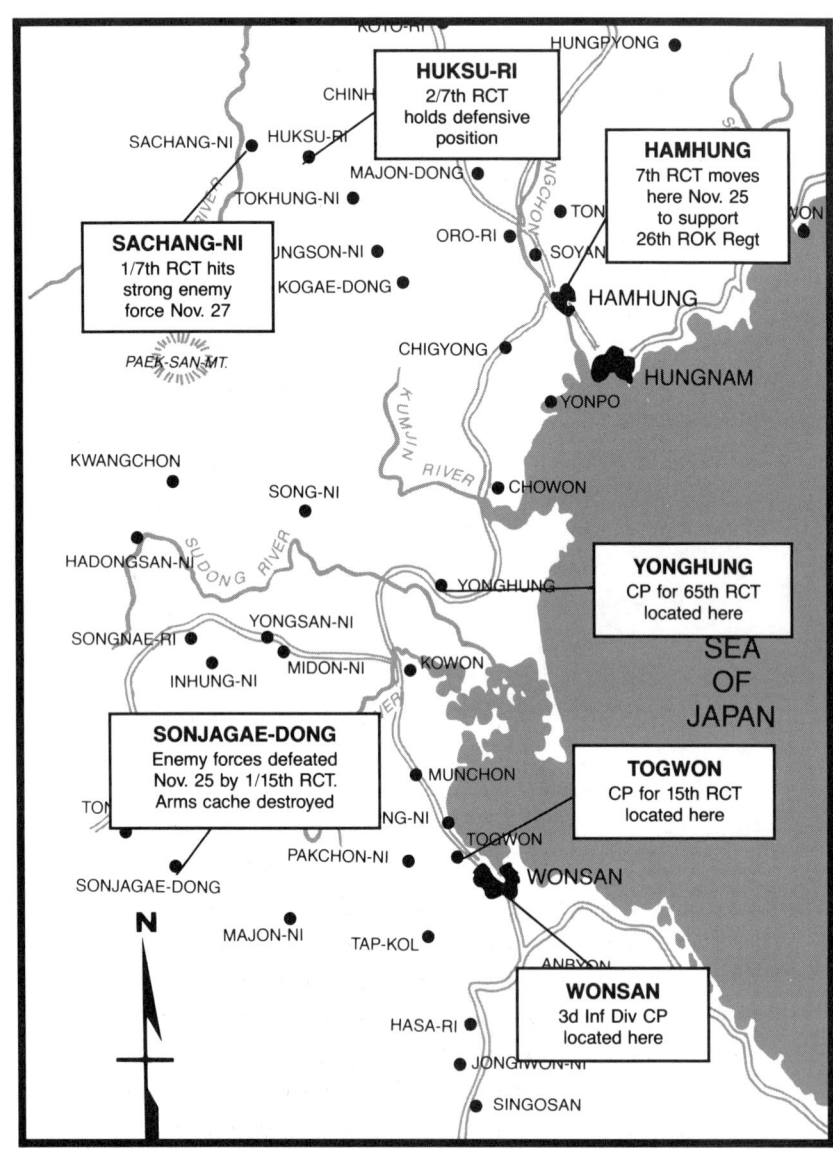

MAP No. 5

Supplies and ammunition were air-dropped; however, a reinforced company from 2/7th Infantry was dispatched for the purpose of pushing through the enemy force and linking up with the beleaguered 1st Battalion.

The fighting was particularly vicious and became deadly hand-to-hand combat where the Charlie Company positions had been penetrated.

By November 30 the fog of war had lifted long enough to make some assessments regarding this renewed enemy action. (See Map 5.)

First, the offensive (referred to by the CCF as their Second Phase Offensive) was general in nature, with troop engagements along the entire U. N. front.

Second, prisoner interrogations confirmed the presence of sufficient CCF formations to establish an estimated enemy strength in excess of 200,000.

Third, the original tactical plan to move the 3d Infantry Division westward over the Taebaek Mountains, establishing physical contact between X Corps and Eighth Army, was no longer feasible (if it had ever been).

A new war had begun.

Notes

1. From the village of Singosan, approximately twenty-two miles south of Wonsan, to a point fifty-three miles northwest of Hamhung, just short of Sachang-ni. This is a straight line

distance of ninety miles from north to south and thirty-five miles from east to west. See Map 3.

2. 3d Infantry Division Command Report (November 1950) placed losses at twenty-eight men, six vehicles, two machine guns, one mortar and one recoilless rifle. Five bodies were recovered two days later.

3. Author interview, BG Robert M. Blanchard, USA (Ret.), March 26, 1990.

4. Author interview, COL Howard B. St. Clair, USA (Ret.), May 16, 1990.

5. See Appleman, *Disaster in Korea*, p. 30.

6

 THE CHINESE INTERVENE

Communist China's hostility toward the United States and American policies in the Far East had its roots in the manner in which, as the Communists perceived it, they were mistreated during World War II.

Despite an inferiority in numbers against the Japanese, Mao Tse-tung and his followers were in many ways more effective in fighting the invaders than Chiang Kai-shek's Kuomintang army. General Joseph W. Stilwell was forced to leave China in 1944 when his forthright views on this subject were made public. And the continuation of lend-lease programs to the Nationalists after V-J Day merely confirmed Mao's suspicions about American duplicity during China's civil strife. By the time of his final victory on the mainland in 1949, America's role as enemy No. One of the People's Republic was etched in stone. Hatred for all things American was a considerable factor in Communist China's decision to intervene in Korea just twelve months later.

Although lacking in much of the equipment of modern warfare, the Chinese forces that entered Korea in the fall of 1950 were veteran troops, well trained and well led. Discipline and confidence have, on many occasions, been decisive factors in battle, and the CCF had both in abundance.[1]

To many Americans who faced him in Korea, the Chinese soldier was the toughest enemy on earth. That opinion was certainly shared by many ROK soldiers who, believing every Chinese to be ten feet tall, fled shamelessly before him.

The Chinese soldier was small by American standards. Except for the Manchurians who were considerably taller, the typical Chinese was barely five feet in height. His body weight averaged between 120 and 130 pounds. He had some elementary school education and was between twenty and twenty-eight years of age. He was most often single and, at the time he entered Korea, had roughly three years of military service behind him. Most of his battlefield experience had come in fighting the Nationalists who, thanks to American largesse, were far better armed and equipped for combat. Some of his comrades did not realize they were fighting beyond the borders of China.

A surprising number (some estimates place it as high as one half) were former Chinese Nationalists who had come over to the Communists, happy to get away from the physical beatings experienced under Chiang Kai-shek. The Chinese soldier's needs were few, living on rice balls and millet, yet he had the stamina to carry loads that would exhaust the average American GI. Clad in a quilted cotton uniform and wearing rubber-soled shoes without socks, he could march twenty miles for fifteen nights in succession through the mountains and valleys of North Korea in subzero weather and still have energy to fight his enemy when the time for combat was at hand.

Brutality toward his enemy was not a common trait, and he sometimes showed a remarkable concern for the wounded. Unlike his North Korean counterpart who often mutilated bodies to make identification difficult, the Chinese frequently marked the American gravesites with the deceased's dog tags.[2]

He was a wily foe, sometimes dragging his own dead and wounded from the battlefield in order to deceive the Americans as to the extent of his losses.[3]

His morale was excellent. The tanks and artillery of the Americans were impressive, but he had confidence in his ability to beat this enemy just as he had beaten the Nationalists.

Some of his determination, however, may have come from external sources. After one ambush in which a large number of CCF were killed, many of the survivors were found to be in such a euphoric state that it was widely believed that hallucinogenic substances were involved.[4]

A serious shortcoming of the CCF was their lack of a modern communications system. Bugles, whistles, shepherd's pipes, and flares were used to signal the attack, seizure of the target, and recall of units. These were not designed for the specific purpose of unnerving the American soldier, but they definitely had that effect.[5] A handicap thus became an asset.

Unlike the North Korean army which was uniformly equipped with Soviet-made armaments, the weaponry of the CCF was an admixture of Japanese, Czech, German, and American origin, most of it having been captured from their enemies. This created an ongoing problem with ammunition supply. It also resulted in an inconsistency in the number of weapons in each organization, some soldiers being armed only with grenades.[6] Having captured numerous weapons and ammunition supplies from the Kuomintang and in their initial onslaught against the ROK and Eighth Army formations in November 1950, the CCF were able to sustain offensive operations into December only as far as the 38th parallel. As it was, the CCF units had to halt every three or four days to replenish supplies of food and ammunition. This enabled Eighth Army to disengage and take up new positions just north of Seoul as the year ended.

In no way, however, did China's entry into the Korean War resemble our own piecemeal fashion. As they say in the hills of Tennessee, the Chinese came in "loaded for bear."

The first Chinese Army units entered Korea on October 18. The 39th and 40th armies crossed the Yalu River at Sinuiju while the 38th and 42nd armies crossed at Manpojin. These units, together with the two armies held in reserve (50th and 66th), comprised the XIII CCF Army Group. Resting in concealed locations by day and marching by night, they took up positions from which they could strike any U.N. force approaching the Manchurian border.

In the Eighth Army sector, CCF troops confronted a battalion of the 2d Regiment, 6th ROK Division (ROK II Corps), south of Pukchin on October 25. The ROK units disintegrated as South Korean soldiers broke and ran. The U.S. 8th Cavalry

The Chinese Intervene

(1st Cavalry Division) was almost destroyed when it was cut off and surrounded in its attempt to bolster the ROK units near Unsan.

To the east, in the X Corps sector, the ROK 3d Division engaged elements of the 42d Army (probably the 124th Division) near Sudong. Prisoners from the 370th Regiment, 124th Division, taken on October 30 by the ROK 26th Regiment, confirmed the presence of integral troop units, not the "patriot volunteers" claimed by China. A series of violent skirmishes developed in each of these areas for the remainder of the month; however, by the end of the first week of November the Chinese formations disappeared just as mysteriously as they had come.

Only later did U.S. analysts learn that this phase of the fighting, referred to by the CCF as their First Phase Offensive (October 25–November 8) was meant to signal China's intent to fight if the United Nations Command persisted in its plans to advance to the Yalu. The signal was misread in Tokyo and in Washington.

As shown in Table 3, each of the six CCF armies was composed of three divisions whose strength was approximately 10,000 each. Thus, a total of 180,000 Chinese soldiers were in North Korea when this new war began.

The 124th Division from the 42nd CCF Army was in the vicinity of the Chosin Reservoir in late October when it engaged the 3d ROK Division and elements of the 7th U.S. Marines. Its sister division, the 126th, remained in reserve but did bump into patrols from the U.S. 7th Infantry Division near the Fusen Reservoir. By mid-November, IX

Table 3

ORGANIZATION OF XIII ARMY GROUP, CHINESE COMMUNIST FORCES

Army	Division	Regiment
38th	112th	334th, 335th, 336th
	113th	337th, 338th, 339th
	114th	340th, 341st, 342nd
39th	115th	343rd, 344th, 345th
	116th	346th, 347th, 348th
	117th	349th, 350th, 351st
40th	118th	352nd, 353rd, 354th
	119th	355th, 356th, 357th
	120th	358th, 359th, 360th
42nd	124th	370th, 371st, 372nd
	125th	373rd, 374th, 375th
	126th	376th, 377th, 378th
50th	148th	442nd, 443rd, 444th
	149th	445th, 446th, 447th
	150th	448th, 440th, 450th
66th	196th	586th, 587th, 588th
	197th	589th, 590th, 591st
	199th	592nd, 593rd, 594th

Source: Montross and Canzona, *U.S. Marine Operations in Korea*, Volume 3, *The Chosin Campaign*, Appendix G, Washington, DC: U.S. Government Printing Office, 1957.

Army Group, Third CCF Field Army, replaced the 42nd Army as the latter moved westward toward the U.S. Eighth Army front. In late November the 89th Division of the 20th CCF Army, moved from Yudam-ni to Sachang-ni in an effort to outflank the 1st Marine Division. As explained earlier, it was

Table 4

ORGANIZATION OF IX ARMY GROUP, CHINESE COMMUNIST FORCES

Army	Division	Regiment
20th	58th	172nd, 173rd, 174th
	59th	175th, 176th, 177th
	60th	178th, 179th, 180th
	89th*	265th, 266th, 267th
26th	76th	226th, 227th, 228th
	77th	229th, 230th, 231st
	78th	232nd, 233rd, 234th
	88th*	262nd, 263rd, 264th
27th	79th	235th, 236th, 237th
	80th	238th, 239th, 240th
	81st	241st, 242nd, 243rd
	90th*	268th, 269th, 270th

Source: Montross and Canzona, *U.S. Marine Operations in Korea*, Volume 3, *The Chosin Campaign*, Appendix G, Washington, DC: U.S. Government Printing Office, 1957.

*Divisions attached from 30th Army as reinforcements for CHOSIN campaign.

engaged and defeated by elements of the 7th Infantry, 3d Infantry Division. The order of battle for IX Army Group is shown in Table 4.

The arrival of these units with an additional 120,000 troops brought the total strength of the CCF in North Korea to approximately 300,000.

Prisoner interrogation and enemy documents captured later in the war indicated that the CCF 58th Division struck the U.S. 1st Marine Division south of Hagaru-ri in early December while the

CCF 60th Division set up roadblocks along the MSR between Hagaru-ri and Chinhung-ni. These units, as well as the 79th and 80th CCF divisions, suffered heavy losses. The latter unit was in action mainly against the 7th Infantry Division's 31st RCT east of the Chosin Reservoir.[7]

The Chinese preferred to fight at night. This tactic maximized their strengths (stamina, stealth, and large numbers) and minimized their weaknesses (susceptibility to air strikes, lack of transport, nonexistent or limited artillery support).

In December 1950 dusk came early in the northern areas of Korea; by 5:30 P.M. there was total darkness. The first three or four hours after nightfall were spent probing and determining the exact location of the American positions, particularly of the automatic weapons. A four- or five-mile march from the assembly area, in columns, brought the first wave of assault troops into position. These troops were lightly armed and equipped, carrying three or four day's rations, a submachine gun and perhaps a dozen hand grenades. They were adept in the use of mortars, and a mortar barrage generally preceded the attack.

On signal—usually a flare, bugle or pipe call—the first wave of attackers would surge forward in an effort to pin the Americans to their position, while other columns attempted to find the weakest point in the line in order to turn a flank or gain a position in the rear of the U.N. forces.

The boundary between adjoining units was most often the weak spot, since each unit, dependent on the support of its neighbor, was understandably reluctant to direct fire on what might be friendly rather than enemy troops. The instinct of self-preservation also made soldiers more inclined to fire across their own front before they would fire in protection of another unit.

The American MLR (main line of resistance) was located behind an OPLR (outpost line of resistance), a position from which early warning of an enemy's advance could be given. This picket line was manned with as few men as possible and had communications back to the MLR (wire, if possible, since the SCR 536 radios were often unreliable in cold weather).[8] The line was located as far forward as possible, yet not so far that the troops manning the OPLR could not be recalled when the enemy forces were deployed for attack. The exact location was obviously dictated by the terrain.[9]

Thus, the stage was set for a military confrontation between the world's most industrialized nation and one of its most primitive societies; between a highly mechanized army and an army of Chinese peasants of whom General Stilwell said, "if properly trained and led, they could be the equal of any in the world."[10]

Notes

1. Members of the United Nations Command referred to the Chinese Army units in Korea as CCF (Chinese Communist Forces). The Chinese, however, invariably referred to these

units as PLA (Peoples Liberation Army), a charade continued throughout the war.

2. Author interview, LTG Pat W. Crizer, USA (Ret.), June 3, 1989.

3. Author interview, BG James O. Boswell, USA (Ret.), June 3, 1989

4. Crizer interview.

5. Crizer interview.

6. Author interview, BG Harley F. Mooney, USA (Ret.), July 26, 1989.

7. Prisoner interrogation provided a remarkably detailed picture of the CCF order of battle during hostilities.

8. As the war progressed and American troops became more sophisticated in the art of war, new techniques were developed. When the SCR 536s were replaced by the ANPRC-6, the obsolete radios were stripped of their receiving mechanism. Wired with their speaker button locked in the "on" position, they were placed under footbridges, along trails, and in abandoned outpost positions and used as a monitoring device. When enemy troops approached, an operator stationed in a listening post and monitoring with earphones could, by closing one switch at a time, determine the location of the enemy. Artillery or mortar fire could then be directed on the enemy position without endangering American lives. Letters, MAJ Joseph J. Piaseczny, USA (Ret.), dated April 4 and October 11, 1990.

9. Author interview, COL Samuel G. Kail, USA (Ret.), March 22, 1990.

10. See Barbara Tuchman, *Stilwell and the American Experience in China, 1911–1945* (New York: Macmillan, 1971).

7

INTO THE ABYSS

At the beginning of December a feeling of apprehension was evident among the American commanders in North Korea. In the chaos of war, it seemed that events had taken on a life of their own. One glance at the division situation map told the story: the map had taken on the appearance of someone with an outbreak of measles.[1]

The 3d Infantry Division's activities during November had been primarily locating and destroying roving bands of guerrillas. Enemy activity had been limited to raiding villages, harrassing supply lines, and making sporadic attacks on outposts. Some of these enemy bands were believed to have as many as 4,000 men and operated mainly in and around villages north of Hamhung (Sinhung), west of Chigyong (Paek-san), south of Wonsan (Anbyon, Hoeyang, and Singosan) as well as at Yangdok on the Majon-ni/Tongyang road west of Wonsan.

The division CP was still located in Wonsan and many of the infantry battalions were situated as much as twenty-five miles from their parent units. The presence of Chinese Communist forces now made it imperative that the 3d Division and other X Corps units be brought closer together to provide mutual support and to prevent infiltration by the enemy.

On November 30 the division was ordered to attack with a strong task force on the Yonghung/Inhung-ni axis and thus assist the Eighth Army by relieving enemy pressure on the EUSAK right flank. The remainder of the division was to be concentrated in the Chigyong/Yonpo area.[2]

X Corps also directed the formation of Task Force Charlie under the command of Brigadier General Armistead D. Mead, assistant division commander. The task force would be under X Corps control and was given the mission of protecting Wonsan and its airfield, and destroying enemy forces within its zone as the division shifted its main body northward.[3]

The 7th RCT was assigned the mission of maintaining blocking positions at Majon-dong, Huksu-ri and Sachang-ni, villages twenty-two, fifty-two and sixty-three miles north and west of Hamhung, respectively.

The 15th RCT moved to Chigyong and was ordered to designate one battalion as division reserve.

The 65th RCT was directed to move to the vicinity of Yonghung and the 64th Heavy Tank Battalion was ordered to position one company in the vicinity of Kowon, to protect the MSR and bridge sites in that area, and to patrol toward the village of Midon-ni, ten miles west of Kowon. Patrols were to be extended in its operational zone to the corps west flank, and the rest of the battalion was to move north to the vicinity of Sinhung-ni, a village midway between Chigyong and Hamhung. Task Force Charlie relieved 3d Division elements in the zone south of Chung-dong, and the division CP moved by motor march to Hamhung, arriving there at 4:00 P.M. on December 1.

2/15th Infantry had been assigned responsibility for protecting the MSR by occupying high ground in the vicinity of Chowon and 3d Recon Company manned outposts west of the MSR from which to give early warning of the advance of any approaching enemy force.

On December 1, X Corps realigned the boundary between 3d and 7th Infantry divisions and ordered the 3d Division to concentrate one RCT near Oro-ri (eight miles north of Hamhung) and another RCT in the vicinity of Chigyong (eight miles south of Hamhung) and to continue to man outpost positions at Huksu-ri and along the Yonghung/Inhung-ni axis.[4] However, before these instructions could be implemented, they were canceled by telephone order and superseded by new instructions. The 3d Division, minus the 7th RCT, was to concentrate in the Wonsan area and to defend the port and airfield, facilities that would be essential to any evacuation plans which might be developed.[5] Accordingly, on this confusing second day of December, Task Force Charlie was dissolved. The 1st KMC Battalion and 3/7th Infantry were detached for assignment to X Corps to cover the withdrawal of corps units north of Hamhung. Upon receiving this order (December 2), the division CP returned to Wonsan by a nine-hour motor march. (See Map 6.)

On December 3 new instructions were received that attached 3/7th Infantry to the 7th Infantry Division for employment near Majon-dong, released

3D INFANTRY DIV. SITUATION MAP

DECEMBER 1 - 4, 1950

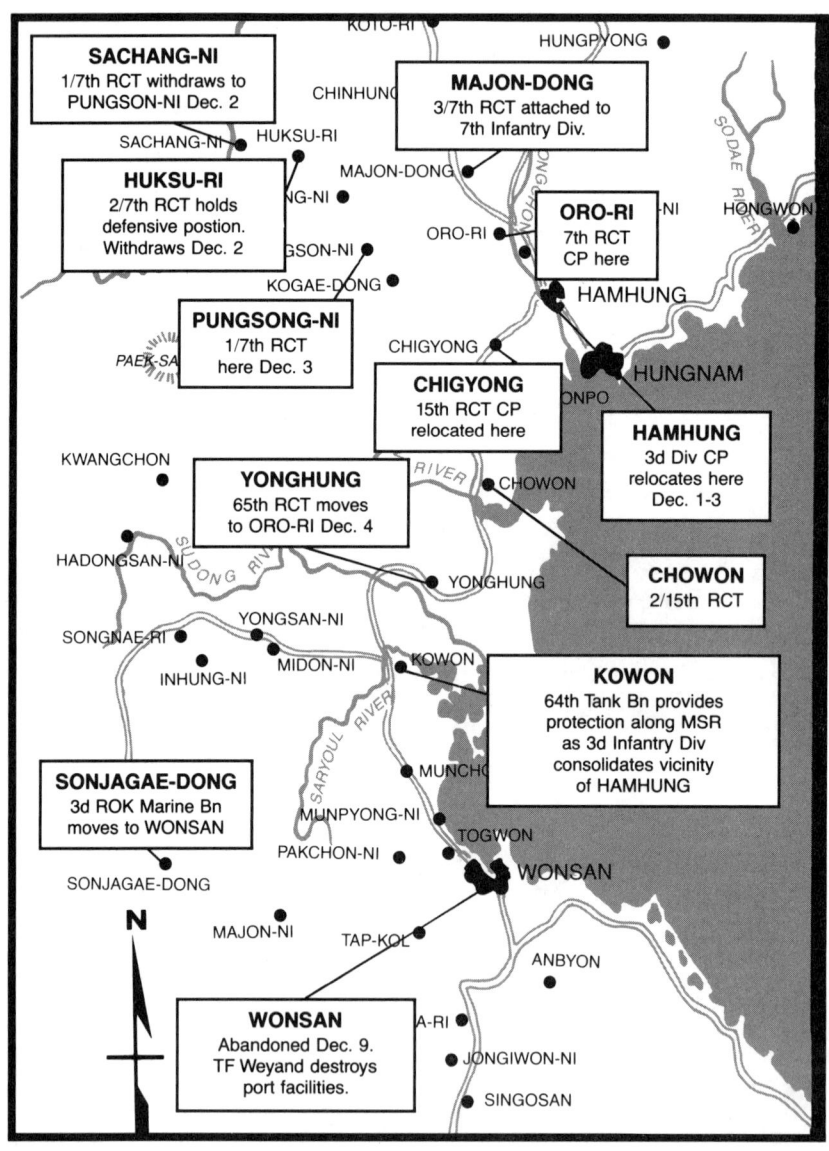

MAP No. 6

the rest of 7th RCT (which had been in corps reserve) to control of 3d Division and once again realigned the boundary between 3d Infantry and 7th Infantry divisions.[6]

Later that same day the division boundary between 3d and 7th divisions was moved for a third time. The division was ordered to relieve the 7th Infantry Division in its operational zone, to concentrate one RCT near Chigyong, to continue the deployment of covering forces along the Chigyong/Huksu-ri and Yonghung/Inhung-ni axes and to protect Yonpo Airfield (about eight miles southeast of Hamhung). 1st KMC Regiment (less 23d Company) was attached to the 3d Division.[7]

While elements of the 3d Division were shuttling back and forth between Wonsan and Hamhung, the division outposts were pulling back from their advanced positions to the west. 3d KMC Battalion withdrew from its patrol base at Tongyang. 1/65th Infantry withdrew from its base near Kwangchon and headed for Wonsan, a move subsequently aborted. 1/7th Infantry began its withdrawal from Sachang-ni at 7:00 A.M. on December 2.

The battalion rearguard was hit by an enemy force (estimated strength of three hundred) and, under intense small-arms fire, withdrew to Huksu-ri. It moved through the positions of 2/7th Infantry at Huksu-ri and continued southeastward about twenty-four miles down the road to establish new defensive positions near Pungson-ni.[8]

Enemy pressure continued to build in front of 2/7th Infantry at Huksu-ri with Fox and George companies suffering heavy casualties. On the morning of December 3 this battalion was ordered to withdraw to new positions on high ground about 1,800 yards south and of Huksu-ri.[9] A heavy fog denied full use of artillery and air support until 11:30 A.M. when improved visibility permitted their use. The 5th KMC Battalion was attached to 7th RCT and joined 2/7th Infantry in position at 10:30 P.M. on December 3.

As directed by X Corps, 65th RCT moved to Oro-ri (eight miles north of Hamhung) and relieved the 7th Division's 32d Infantry Regiment on December 4. With the relief of the 32d Infantry, 3/7th Infantry and 3/15th Infantry were attached to 65th RCT.[10]

2/65th Infantry remained near Yonghung until all division units had cleared its position in the movement north to Hamhung, except for the 64th Heavy Tank Battalion. The tank battalion (less Company B) then fell in behind 2/65th Infantry and on December 5 was the last divisional unit to move up the Wonsan/Hamhung MSR.

As the last elements of the division departed Wonsan on December 4, Task Force Weyand under the command of LTC Fred C. Weyand, division deputy chief of staff, was left behind to secure the port and airfield until all personnel, vehicles, and supplies (i.e., ammunition and petroleum products) not essential to the Hungnam operation could be removed by sea. This security force was composed of Company B, 64th Heavy Tank Battalion; 1st and 3d KMC battalions; one platoon from 3d Recon Company; one platoon from Mortar Company, 15th Infantry; one platoon from 3d AAA AW Battalion; and a detachment from 3d Signal Company. A shore party group from the 1st Marine Division assisted these units in outloading all cargo and approximately 7,000 civilians aboard LSTs (landing ship, tanks). This operation was completed December 9. The port facilities and other installations of military value were then destroyed by explosive charges.

The fierce fighting taking place in the sector assigned to the 1st Marine Division north of Hamhung and reports of the annihilation of the 7th Infantry Division's 31st RCT east of the Chosin Reservoir made it abundantly clear that hard days lay ahead. Close coordination between all units would be essential if the troops in northeast Korea were to escape the trap now being sprung by the Chinese Communist forces that had taken over from the NKPA the primary role in fighting the United Nations Command.

The marine division had fought off hordes of Chinese (some estimates placed it at eight CCF divisions; others placed it even higher). They had consolidated their units at Hagaru-ri and were preparing to fight their way south to Koto-ri. It would have been impossible for any organization, even well-trained marines, to fight its way to the sea, fifty-three miles from Koto-ri, without out the help of their comrades-in-arms. By a stroke of good fortune, the fresh, relatively full-strength 3d Infantry Division was in position to come north, link up with the marine division and hold open the tenuous road to the sea.[11] General Almond, during a visit to the 3d Division CP, discussed with General Soule the plight of the marine division. The corps commander then returned to his headquarters and issued orders putting this critical operation in motion.

At 8:30 P.M. on December 5, the 3d Division formed Task Force Dog, with instructions that it be ready to move on six hours' notice. On order the task force was to proceed to Majon-dong, twenty-two miles northwest Hamhung, and provide cover for the marine division as far north as Chinhung-ni (thirteen miles north of Majon-dong).[12] The marine division had consolidated its units at Koto-ri (ten miles north of Chinhung-ni) and would attempt to break through the CCF blocking positions known to be along the MSR south of Koto-ri. (See Map 7.)

Brigadier General Armistead D. Mead was selected to lead Task Force Dog; it was an assignment that a fighter like "Red" Mead lived for.

The task force was composed of:

3/7th Infantry
92d Armored F/A Battalion
Platoon, 3d Recon Company
Co A, 73d Engineer (C) Bn
52d Transportation Truck Bn
Det, Ord Bomb Disposal Unit
Det, 3d Signal Company
Det, Tactical Air Control Party

Headquarters 3d AAA AW Battalion was also assigned to the task force to provide additional mobility and firepower.[13] It would also serve as the task force headquarters (General Mead was accompanied by his aide, 1st Lt Harley F. Mooney).

Under Division Operations Order No. 4, which implemented the corps directive, 65th RCT was ordered to release 3/7th Infantry to the control of the task force commander upon request, to man strong

3D INFANTRY DIV. SITUATION MAP

DECEMBER 5 - 10, 1950

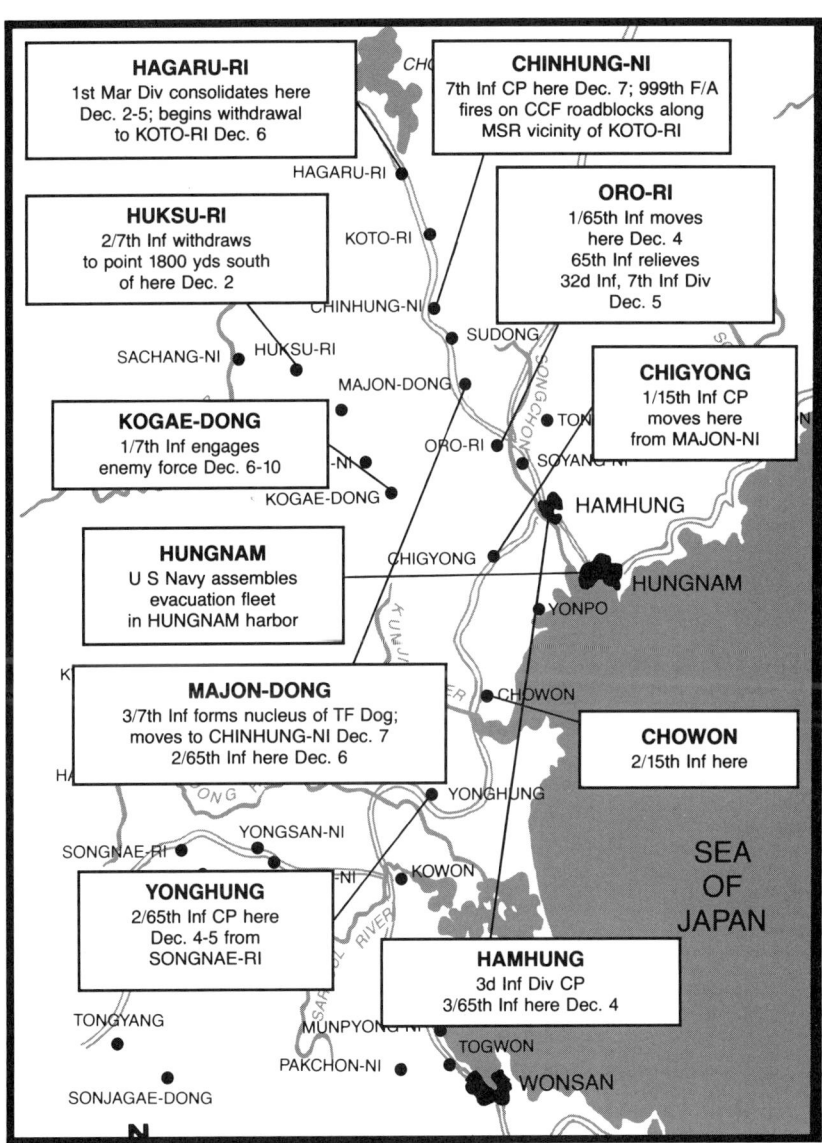

MAP No. 7

defensive positions along the ridgelines in the vicinity of Majon-dong and provide covering fire for Task Force Dog as it moved up the MSR to Chinhung-ni. Division Artillery (DivArty) was ordered to provide aerial observation and artillery support with the 31st Field Artillery, which was attached to the 3d Division for this mission.

Shortly after midnight on December 6–7, X Corps activated the task force. It departed Majon-dong at 11:00 A.M. and arrived at Chinhung-ni at 2:20 P.M. on December 7, relieving the 1st Battalion, 1st Marine Regiment and enabling that unit to strike north on the MSR in an effort to aid the marine column coming south from Koto-ri.

The 999th Armored Field Artillery with its self-propelled 155mm howitzers moved into position to fire in support of the task force. Its commander, LTC Kenneth Dawalt, remembered it as one of his greatest risks, firing an artillery barrage at the Chinese over the heads of the marines and parallel to the road, with charge 7, the maximum load for 155s. "An error in deflection would have killed our own troops. I got a few gray hairs that night."[14]

The marines, with attached army troops, fought their way clear of the CCF roadblocks, and the leading elements of their column reached the task force positions at Chinhung-ni at 2:45 A.M. on December 10.[15] The marine column continued south and was temporarily halted at a point near Sudong (six miles south of Chinhung-ni) where an estimated two hundred enemy troops attacked Company G, 65th Infantry. The enemy was repulsed and the marine column continued to move toward

Hamhung. Later that day a second enemy attack at Sudong was repulsed by the 65th Infantry.

At 4:50 A.M. on December 11, a third attack at Sudong was beaten off by the 65th Infantry; however, this attack succeeded in destroying several vehicles and disrupting the evacuation process for a short period.

The entire Marine column cleared Chinhung-ni at 1:35 P.M. on December 11 and cleared Majon-dong at 4:30 P.M. the same day. Task Force Dog returned to Majon-dong at 8:00 P.M. that same evening and was disbanded, with its component units reverting to parent unit control.[16]

The final stage of the Hungnam operation began the following morning (December 12) with the establishment of the outer defensive line around the Hamhung/Hungnam perimeter. Line Charlie was manned by 3d Infantry Division troops on the left (southwest) and 7th Infantry Division troops on the right (northeast).

Notes

1. The color red was used to depict the location of enemy forces on military situation maps.

2. X Corps Operations Order No. 6, November 30, 1950.

3. Primary source document for this portion of the narrative is Command Report, 3d Infantry Division for December 1950, on file at the U.S. Army Center for Military History, Carlisle Barracks, PA. Copy in author's possession. Also, author interviews of BG Blanchard and Colonels Kail and St. Clair cited elsewhere.

4. X Corps Operations Instructions No. 20 (December 1, 1950).

5. X Corps Operations Instructions No. 21 (December 2, 1950).

6. X Corps Operations Instructions No. 23 (December 3, 1950).

7. X Corps Operations Instructions No. 24 (December 3, 1950).

8. Five M4AE tanks and one M2 dozer tank could not be moved over the icy roads from Pungson-ni in the withdrawal to Chigyong. These vehicles were destroyed. (3d Inf Div Command Rpt—December 1950).

9. Although the official records place the distance at 4,000 yards, I have accepted Colonel Kail's estimate of 1,800 yards, since he was present at the time.

10. X Corps Operations Instructions No. 24 (December 3, 1950).

11. The brevity of these comments regarding the withdrawal of the 1st Marine Division should not be interpreted as a lack of appreciation for what they did. Their story has been told admirably in a number of publications; this narrative deals with the 3d Infantry Division and its accomplishments in the Hungnam operation. For a detailed account of the 1st Marine Division in northeast Korea, the serious student of military history will want to read: Montross and Canzona, *U.S. Marine Operations in Korea*, Volume 3: *The Chosin Campaign* (Washington: GPO, 1957); and Hammel, *Chosin—Heroic Ordeal* (New York: Vanguard Press, 1981).

12. X Corps Operations Instructions No. 26 (December 5, 1950).

13. Company A, 10th Engineer (C) Bn was added to the task force when it became obvious that road and bridge repair capabilities would be needed.

14. Letter to author, BG Kenneth F. Dawalt, USA (Ret.), dated Feb. 21, 1989. The 155s had a maximum range of approximately ten miles. However, extremely cold weather often caused the rounds to fall short.

15. Army troops included the survivors of the 7th Division's ill-fated 31st RCT that had been decimated east of the Chosin Reservoir, and Company D, 10th Engineer (C) Battalion, a unit organic to the 3d Infantry Division. On November 27 this unit, under the command of Captain Phillip A. Kulbes, was ordered by X Corps to proceed to Hagaru-ri and begin construction of a

forward command post for X Corps. When the Chinese cut the road south of Hagaru-ri, Company D was attached to 3/1st Marines and fought as infantrymen on the withdrawal south to Chinhung-ni. The company returned to 3d Division control on December 13 and was subsequently awarded a Presidential Unit Citation for its performance under enemy fire.

16. The 1st Marine Division has been justly lauded for this magnificent endeavor. However, one of the myths that has grown up around the breakout is that it fought its way virtually unaided to the sea at Hungnam. In fact, its combat role ended when it entered the 3d Division defensive perimeter at Chinhung-ni, a distance of forty-three miles from the sea. Chinhung-ni is thirty-five miles south of Yudam-ni, the point at which the marine withdrawal began.

3D INFANTRY DIV. SITUATION MAP

DECEMBER 11 - 16, 1950

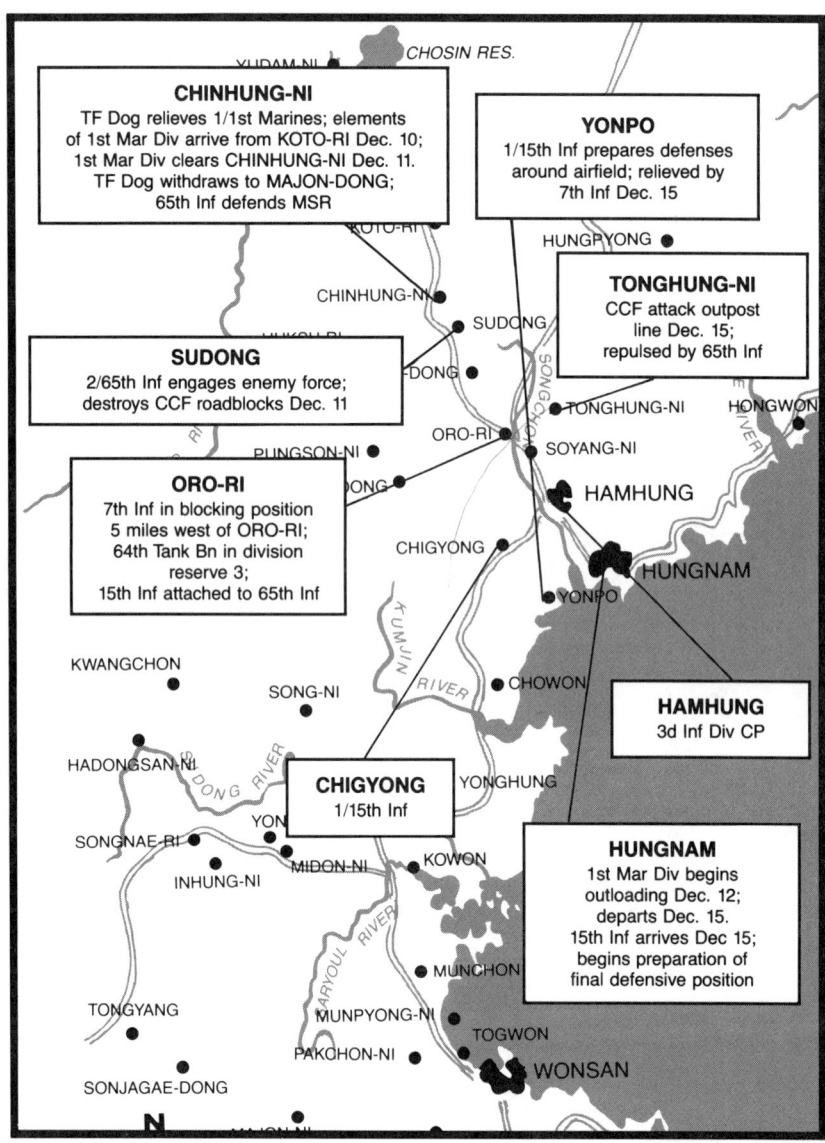

MAP No. 8

8

 Trading Space for Time

On Tuesday, December 12, 3d Division Operations Order No. 5 promulgated instructions under which all division units would function from the time of withdrawal from positions north of Hamhung through the evacuation of all U.N. forces from Hungnam.

The regimental combat teams were dissolved. 7th Infantry occupied a blocking position roughly five miles due west of Oro-ri. 65th Infantry would cover the area four miles northwest of Oro-ri on the road to Majon-dong. On order, each regiment would withdraw to Line Charlie and tie in with units from the 7th Infantry Division on the right, or northeast, end of the perimeter. (See Map 8.)[1]

Centered on Hungnam and extending in progressively smaller arcs from the sea southwest of Hungnam to the water's edge northeast of that city, a series of phase lines was established for the defense of the United Nations perimeter during the final troop withdrawal. Line Charlie, the outermost line, was roughly one mile south of the village of Oro-ri (eight miles north of Hamhung. This included an area with a depth of fifteen miles (from Hungnam) and a width of approximately twenty-two miles; an overall area of 330 square miles. Line

Tare, two to three miles behind Line Charlie, continued to include the city of Hamhung but reduced the perimeter, leaving an area of roughly 260 square miles. Line Mike, two to three miles behind Line Tare, further reduced the perimeter, comprising an area of 200 square miles. It was at Line Peter that Hamhung was abandoned. The perimeter was reduced to an area of approximately 150 square miles, having a width of twenty-one miles and a depth of seven miles. Line Able was considerably closer to the sea, and withdrawal to this line reduced the area by slightly more than one half, to approximately 60 square miles. Line Able permitted the continued use of Yonpo Airfield which was roughly five miles southwest of Hungnam. Line Fox, the final defensive line, consisted of most of the city of Hungnam and extended inland for roughly two and a half miles; thus the final perimeter was slightly less than 25 square miles.

General Soule's tactical concept, which made use of the control lines (Queen, King, George) on the southwest end of the perimeter, enabled him to withdraw elements of the 3d Division on the left flank as he deemed necessary, while retaining positions on the right which included the final fallback position.

3/7th Infantry was assigned as division reserve; 15th Infantry, in corps reserve, was ordered to prepare positions on the main line of resistance (MLR) and to occupy the line on order, when released from corps reserve.

The 1st Korean Marine Corps Battalion, attached to the 3d Division, prepared defensive positions on the left flank at the outermost line and prepared to turn the position over to the 7th Infantry and withdraw on order, for embarkation.[2]

Meanwhile, 3d Recon Company was given the mission of screening the division front on the Hamhung/Oro-ri and Hamhung/Sinhung-ni approaches and also of protecting communications lines from sabotage.

The 64th Heavy Tank Battalion was ordered into division reserve and directed to prepare plans for counterattack, if ordered, in the center sector occupied by the 65th Infantry.

All units were ordered to conduct aggressive forward patrolling and to deny passage to civilians attempting to enter the perimeter. Antipersonnel mines were laid, demolition charges prepared and withdrawals were to be made on division order only. (See Map 9.)

Checkpoints and guard posts were established in Hamhung and personnel from the 3d CIC (counterintelligence corps) and 3d Military Police Company worked with civil assistance teams from division headquarters in screening the thousands of civilians who were attempting to leave North Korea before the communist forces arrived. Some weapons and ammunition caches were found, and more than one hundred guerrillas were taken prisoner.

Company B, 7th Infantry was attacked at 7:30 A.M. on December 13 by approximately two hundred enemy troops supported by artillery and mortar fire. After a four-hour firefight this enemy force was dispersed with the aid of air support. Approximately fifty enemy troops were killed. This was the first reported incident in the 3d Division sector in which en-

3D INFANTRY DIV. SITUATION MAP

DECEMBER 17 - 22, 1950

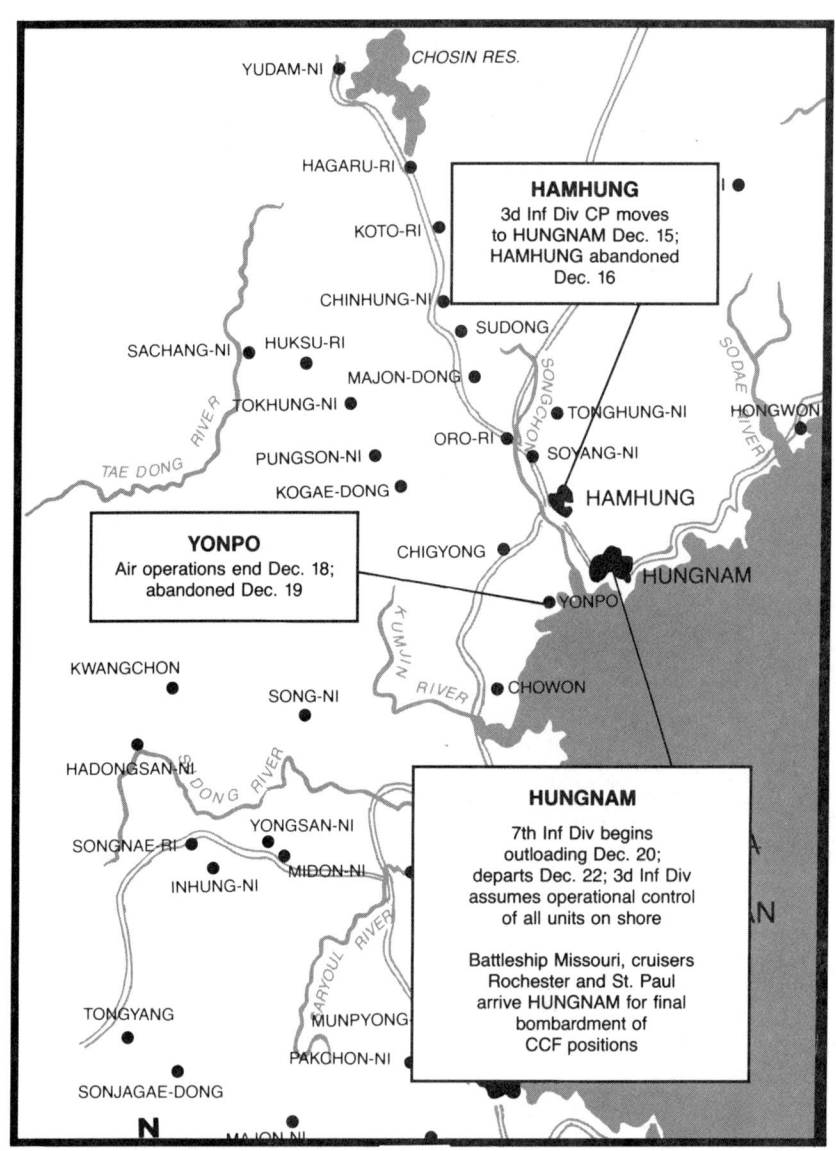

MAP No. 9

emy troops wore American uniforms. Company B, supported by Company F, 7th Infantry, withdrew to new positions at 3:00 P.M. Covering fire from the 10th Field Artillery Battalion killed twenty-five enemy who were engaged in harassing fire.

With the 15th Infantry still in corps reserve, the corps commander elected to divide the regiment into battalion-sized components. LTC Blanchard's 1/15th Infantry, occupying positions in the 7th Infantry's zone, was attached to that regiment. LTC Peck's 2/15th Infantry remained in corps reserve but moved from its position north of Hamhung to the outskirts of Hungnam. LTC Farrell's 3/15th Infantry replaced 2/15th Infantry north of Hamhung and was attached to the 65th Infantry until relieved by that regiment's own 3d Battalion on December 17. (See Map 10.)

The 10th, 39th, and 58th Field Artillery battalions, 999th Armored Field Artillery and 3d AAA AW Battalion, all organic to the division, had rendered superb support to the three infantry regiments in the short time they had been in Korea. They would now prove their worth once again by their performance in the Hungnam operation.

Although normal procedure called for the assignment of an artillery battalion to fire in direct support of a specific infantry regiment on a more or less permanent basis (thus creating a bond of understanding and awareness), the ever-shrinking perimeter would enable the artillerymen to employ the technique of "cross-registration" of artillery pieces. In brief, each battalion would use one field piece to "register" on a target in the area assigned to the artillery battalion adjacent to its own. This would facilitate the rapid shifting of fire, if it became necessary, from one artillery battalion fire zone to the neighboring zone by using the firing coordinates of the artillery piece previously cross-registered.

The 105mm and 155mm howitzer battalions had the range to provide artillery support anywhere it was needed as the perimeter began to contract. Corps artillery was equipped with eight-inch guns; naval gunfire from the USS *Rochester* and the USS *St. Paul* (eight-inch guns) was available and the sixteen-inch guns of the USS *Missouri*, which was also on station, could reach out to distances of twenty-four miles.

Indirect fire was effective, not only in breaking up enemy troop concentrations, but also in its ability to illuminate the battlefield at night with starshells and to disrupt the advance of enemy units as they pressed their attacks on the defensive perimeter.

The CCF crept closer and shortly after midnight on December 13–14, to the accompaniment of blaring bugles, struck Line Charlie occupied by 1/65th Infantry at Oro-ri. One platoon of Company B was overrun and temporarily forced to give ground. A counterattack at daybreak by Companies B and C, supported by artillery and air support, restored the line. The enemy withdrew.

A test of General Soule's flexibility came swiftly and in an unexpected area when the CCF suddenly shifted pressure to the village of Tonghung-ni about four miles east and slightly north of Oro-ri. Company I, 65th Infantry, outposting the King-Charlie Line, was hit by an estimated two hundred Chinese and, after a hot firefight, was ordered to pull back to the King-Tare line. This occurred at 1:00 A.M. on December 15. Enemy losses were believed to be high, as judged by prisoner interrogation.

At midnight on December 14–15, division headquarters ordered the withdrawal of the 7th and 65th Infantry regiments to the Peter and Able Lines beginning at 8:00 A.M. on the 16th. Covering forces were to remain on the Queen-King-George-Tare Line until noon on December 16. This had the effect of shortening the defensive lines on the left side of the perimeter which had been weakened by the withdrawal of the 1st KMC Battalion.[3]

At about this same time, enemy formations were hitting LTC Kail's 2/7th Infantry occupying the King-Tare Line but outposting the King-Charlie Line. The battalion, reinforced by companies B and C from the 1st battalion, had five platoons on the line—one from each company. CCF units in battalion strength hit the outpost positions of Company G. The battle raged from 3:00 A.M. to 7:30 A.M. and the enemy was beaten off. The fight then shifted to the Company B outpost, where the enemy pressed the attack for four hours. This platoon was surrounded but fought its way back to the company MLR with the aid of artillery and supporting armor.

Meanwhile, the enemy began to hammer at the defenses of Company L, 7th Infantry. Line Charlie was no longer tenable.

A briefing at X Corps headquarters was conducted this same day for staff members of the 3d and 7th Infantry divisions. 3d Division, after occupying Line Able on December 16, would fall back to Line Fox on the following day and cover the withdrawal of the 7th Division to the embarkation point. At the request of LTC Hoskot, 3d Division G–3, the order was amended to permit the retention of Line Able until such time as the enemy forced its abandonment. This would enable the 3d Division to retain the initiative and deny the enemy an opportunity to bring the entire beachhead under direct mortar fire, a weapon the CCF used with commendable proficiency.[4]

The division CP moved from Hamhung to Hungnam at noon on December 15. That afternoon 2/7th Infantry pulled back under continuous pressure to positions on the King-George-Mike Line. At the time this action was taking place on the left, 3/65th Infantry on the right was executing a withdrawal to the King-Mike Line.[5] Once again the enemy shifted his forces and began probing in front of 1/15th Infantry, still attached to the 7th Infantry. At 4:40 A.M. on December 16, 1/15th Infantry repulsed a CCF attack. It covered the withdrawal of 2/7th Infantry to Line Able and then made its own withdrawal at 5:00 P.M. Upon crossing the Songchon River, 1/15th reverted to 15th Infantry control.

Enemy pressure continued throughout the day, but artillery fire discouraged close pursuit. In coordination with this attack, the Chinese struck 3/65th Infantry on Line Mike. A breakthrough occurred and a counterattack by the battalion reserve was necessary to restore the line shortly after daybreak. Twenty-seven prisoners were taken and enemy losses were believed to be heavy.

Major General Edward M. Almond (center), Commanding General of X Corps. The officer on the left is Captain Alexander M. Haig, General Almond's aide. 1st Lieutenant Robert J. St. Aubin, General Almond's pilot, is on the right. U.S. Army Photo 111-SC-356722, courtesy of National Archives.

Major General Edward M. Almond, (left) X Corps commander, awarding the Distinguished Service Cross to Major General Robert H. Soule in recognition of his outstanding performance in executing the withdrawal from North Korea. Brigadier General Armistead D. Mead (right), the Assistant Division Commander, received the Silver Star for his accomplishments in command of Task Force Dog, the relief column sent to Chinhung-ni to link up with the 1st Marine Division as it fought its way south from the Chosin Reservoir. The link-up between Marine and Army units occurred 43 miles from the sea. U.S. Army Photo 111-SC-355389, courtesy of National Archives.

Members of the Navy's Underwater Demolition Team unload C–3 explosives on the dock at Hungnam. The port facilities were demolished after the withdrawal of the last 3d Division troops from the beachhead. U.S. Army Photo 111–SC–354898, courtesy of National Archives.

Smoke billows hundreds of feet in the air as the last troops of the 3d Infantry Division withdraw from the Hungnam beachhead in North Korea on December 24, 1950. U.S. Army Photo 111-SC-355428, courtesy of National Archives.

USS *Begor* (APD-127) passes in the foreground in Hungnam harbor on December 24, 1950, as huge explosions rip the harbor installation. U.S. Navy Photo 80-C-424297, courtesy of National Archives.

Last photo of Major General Robert H. Soule, taken in November 1951, shortly after his return to the United States. He died in Washington, DC, on January 19, 1952, less than two months after this picture was taken. U.S. Army Photo 111–P–19888, courtesy of National Archives.

7th and 65th Infantry were ordered to withdraw to Line Fox beginning at 9:00 A.M. on December 17. This movement was to be completed by 5:00 P.M. the same day, with strong outposts remaining on Line Able.[6]

The 15th Infantry continued to prepare Line Fox while the 10th Engineer (C) Battalion destroyed road and rail bridges in the abandoned area with time delay fuses. Covering forces temporarily remained on lines Queen-King-George-Able until noon and then rejoined the main body, thus permitting the continued use of Yonpo Airfield for air evacuation.

The division reserve (3/7th Infantry and the 64th Heavy Tank Battalion) moved northeast of the Songchon River to be nearer the main line of resistance (MLR).

By nightfall on December 16 all three infantry regiments had withdrawn to Line Able, with outposts on Line Peter. The abandonment of Line Mike marked the evacuation of Hamhung, now mostly in ruins.

By mid-afternoon on December 17, the 7th and 65th Infantry Regiments had withdrawn to Line Fox and established strong outposts on Line Able. 1/65th Infantry relieved 17th Infantry on Line Able, and 3/65th Infantry relieved 3/32d Infantry. The 15th Infantry, scheduled to revert to 3d Division control on December 17, was ordered to man outposts on Line Able in the 7th Division zone on the northeast bank of the Songchon River and to assume responsibility for relieving all 7th Division troops on December 18.

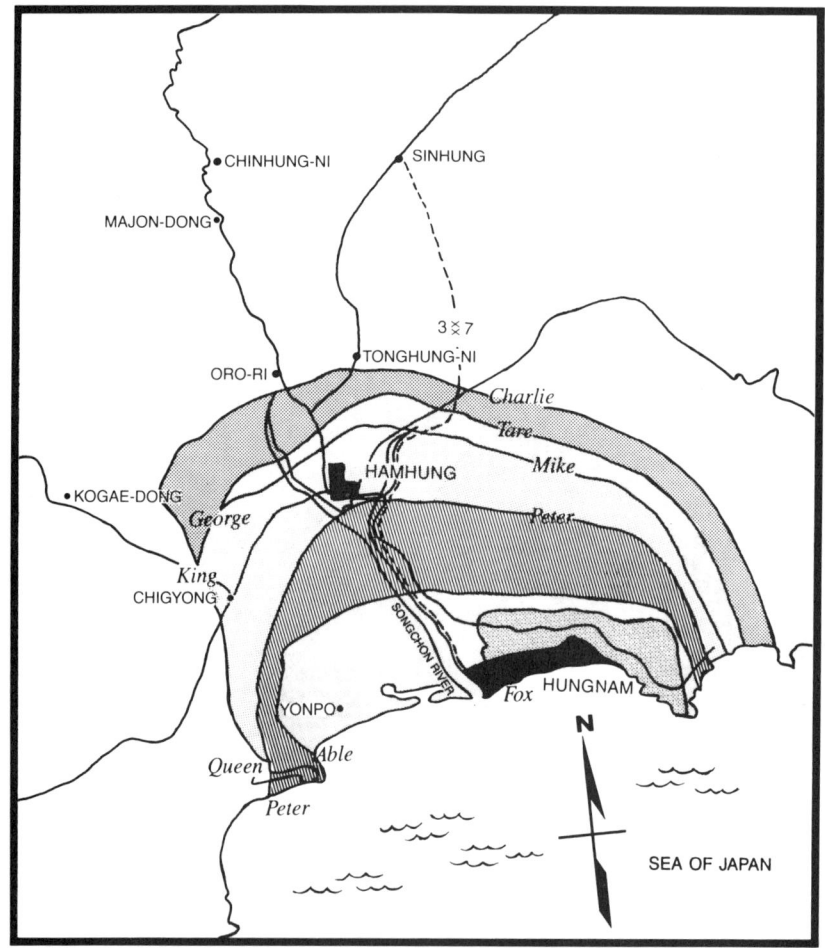

MAP No. 10 - Northeast Korea, Phase Lines at Hungnam

Most withdrawals were conducted during daylight hours. This practice took advantage of the enemy's inability or unwillingness to mount offensive operations in daylight when observed gunfire (from artillery and naval vessels offshore) could do the greatest damage to troop concentrations. Nevertheless, deception was used to the utmost, with the covering force remaining on each phase line and making a show of strength until dusk. The covering force was then withdrawn after dusk and listening posts were left in position to call in artillery fire on the positions just vacated.

Since their gun tubes could not be sufficiently elevated to deliver high-angle fire, the tanks of the 64th Heavy Tank Battalion were phased out of the defensive perimeter over a three-day period. Company C was outloaded on December 17, followed by Company A on December 20. The rest of the battalion (less Company B, still attached to 7th Infantry) departed on December 21.

Encouraged by the cautious approach of the CCF units, General Almond, the corps commander, decided on December 17 to amend his order relieving the 7th Division of assignment in the perimeter. The 15th Infantry was released from X Corps reserve at 4:30 P.M. on December 17 and placed under operational control of the 7th Infantry Division. 1/15th Infantry was struck shortly after midnight on December 17–18, by five hundred Chinese well supported by mortars and automatic weapons. The enemy broke contact after three hours, leaving approximately seventy dead on the battalion front. Twenty-three prisoners were taken.

1/15th Infantry covered the withdrawal of 2/7th Infantry to Line Able on December 19 and then made its own withdrawal at 5:00 P.M. Upon crossing the Songchon River, 1/15th Infantry reverted to control of the 15th Infantry.

Artillery battalions from the 7th Division were placed under control of the 3d Division to reinforce the fire of the direct support battalions. The 15th AAA AW Battalion joined the organic 3d AAA AW Battalion in the 3d Division sector, effectively doubling the firepower available from these automatic weapons with their awesome rate of fire.

Early on the morning of December 18 approximately twenty-five enemy attacked the perimeter at the point marking the boundary between companies E and G of the 15th Infantry. The attack was repulsed. A short while later an estimated fifty enemy troops broke through the right flank of Company I, 15th Infantry, but the position was restored by noon. Eight of the enemy were killed in this action.

Plans having been finalized the previous day, the relief of the 7th Infantry Division was completed on December 19. The 7th and 65th Infantry regiments relieved the 32d Infantry. 3/65th Infantry, still on Line Able east of the Songchon River, was placed under 7th Division control pending arrival at Line Fox. The 17th Infantry was placed under 3d Infantry Division control pending its departure with other 7th Division units. Also, the 15th Infantry reverted to 3d Division control.

The 65th Infantry completed the relief of the 17th Infantry at noon on December 20 and assumed responsibility for the entire 7th Division sector. All

7th Division units reverted to that division's control and outloading began on December 21. Control of X Corps troops remaining on shore passed to the commanding general of the 3d Infantry Division on December 20. The embarkation process proceeded in an orderly manner despite a sudden drop in the temperature to subzero readings (-5° F.) that was accompanied by high winds and rough seas. As night fell on December 22, General Soule's 3d Infantry Division was alone on the shore.

Notes

1. References to phase lines Able, Charlie, Fox, George, King and Mike are extensive in chapter 8. In order to avoid confusion, all references in this chapter to rifle and weapons companies have used the unit's letter designation (Company "C," 15th Infantry) rather than the phonetic alphabet ("Charlie Company," 15th Infantry).

2. This unit moved to Yonpo Airfield for air evacuation on December 13.

3. 3d Inf Div Operations Instructions No. 4 (December 13, 1950).

4. In the fighting on and after December 4, enemy troop units assaulting the 3d Infantry Division lines were identified as the 20th, 26th, and 27th CCF Armies as well as the 1st and 3d NKPA Divisions that had somehow managed to regroup after their defeat at Pyongyang in October.

5. The combat action described here and all subsequent action in the narrative is based on information contained in the regimental command reports for the 7th, 15th and 65th Infantry Regiments for December 1950, on file at the U.S. Army Center for Military History, Carlisle Barracks, PA. Copies are in the author's possession.

6. 3d Inf Div Operations Instructions No. 6 (December 16, 1950).

9

 DELIVERANCE

By the morning of December 22, the area within the defensive perimeter at Hungnam had shrunk to an estimated twelve square miles. 2/65th Infantry moved from Line Peter to Line Able and prepared to cover the withdrawal of 1/65th Infantry and 3/65th Infantry to Line Fox. This move was scheduled for execution on December 23 unless enemy pressure forced an earlier decision.

An uncharacteristic calm descended upon the battlefield, and no enemy activity was reported in the sectors occupied by the 7th and 15th Infantry. Since it is critical in a retrograde movement to maintain contact with the enemy in order to avoid unpleasant surprises, a patrol of squad strength was sent out by the 15th Infantry to probe for the exact location of enemy forces. This force encountered an enemy patrol at a distance of approximately one thousand yards from Line Peter. The enemy patrol was not aggressive, seemingly content merely to keep the American MLR under observation. A base of fire was laid down and the enemy patrol withdrew. An enemy probe was detected later during the day in front of Company F, 15th Infantry, but it, too, withdrew when fired upon.

On the night of December 22 an estimated one hundred and twenty-five enemy troops made an attack against a roadblock in front of 3/15th Infantry, along a section of the left flank occupied by Company L, 15th Infantry. Tanks from the regimental tank company and infantry manning the roadblock withdrew to prepared positions and called in artillery and AAA gunfire. A counterattack then succeeded in driving off the enemy whose losses were estimated at thirty killed and one wounded prisoner.

After making one last effort to interfere with the evacuation process on the night of December 22–23, most of the fight seemed to go out of the enemy force along the defensive perimeter. They had either been literally shelled into a state of shock by the pounding from air strikes, artillery, and naval gunfire, or they were physically spent and low on food and ammunition.

As a result, withdrawal operations conformed to plan and proceeded unhampered on December 23 with 1/65th Infantry and 3/65th Infantry making scheduled withdrawals to Line Fox.

The 39th Field Artillery laid down fire in the sectors occupied by 2/15th Infantry and 3/15th Infantry while Tank Company, 15th Infantry, was outloaded during daylight hours.

Artillery and naval gunfire continued to pound away at the enemy on the night of December 23, with starshells from the ships illuminating the battlefield and high explosive shells from the artillery battalions battering enemy troop positions.

As dawn broke in the eastern sky on Christmas Eve, there were still about 9,000 Americans

Table 5
TROOP STRENGTH OF INFANTRY BATTALIONS—DECEMBER 24, 1950

	Officers	Warrant Officers	Enlisted Men
1/7th Infantry	28	04	550
2/7th Infantry	27	04	450
3/7th Infantry	32	04	646
1/15th Infantry	34	04	552
2/15th Infantry	23	04	580
3/15th Infantry	34	03	789
1/65th Infantry	28	04	836
2/65th Infantry	31	05	842
3/65th Infantry	28	04	857

Source: Morning Report, WD AGO Form 1, for December 24, 1950. On file at Military Personnel Records Center, St. Louis, MO.

on shore in the Hungnam beachhead. The troop strength of the infantry battalions on this final day of military operations in Northeast Korea is shown in Table 5.

General Almond left his corps headquarters aboard the USS *Mount McKinley* at 9:15 A.M. and went ashore to observe the final preparations for the departure from the beachhead. One of his last acts in North Korea was to present the Distinguished Service Cross (the nation's second highest award for valor) to General Soule for his performance in guiding the 3d Infantry Division so skillfully through its baptism of fire.[1]

As the defensive perimeter contracted in successive moves back to the water's edge, each of the division's infantry regiments (7th, 15th, and 65th) reduced its position to a battalion-sized front.

The tempo of activity increased and tension mounted as the noon hour approached. The Chinese were unable to penetrate the curtain of steel laid down by the navy.

Only one mishap occurred when a driver from the amphibious tractor battalion carelessly tossed a cigarette butt onto a stack of 4,000 rounds of mortar ammunition. One officer and five enlisted marines were killed by the explosion.[2]

As the USS *Missouri* stood out to sea, destroyers from the naval armada off shore moved in to provide the final bombardment to cover the troop withdrawals.

The division covering force consisted of Company B, 64th Heavy Tank Battalion (attached to 7th Infantry for this final operation), elements of 3d Recon Company and automatic weapons from 3d AAA AW Battalion (eight self-propelled quad .50s and twenty-four self-propelled twin 40s). This force retired from Line Fox at 9:30 A.M.[3]

Colonel Guthrie's 7th Infantry occupied the southwestern end of the perimeter and would withdraw over Pink Beach. Since this beach was somewhat isolated from the other beaches by the presence of a loading dock or pier that jutted out from shore (see Map 11), initial withdrawal had to be made at that end of the line.

The 58th Armored Field Artillery normally fired in support of the 65th Infantry; however, since its self-propelled guns could not be elevated sufficiently to deliver a high-angle, plunging fire, it was

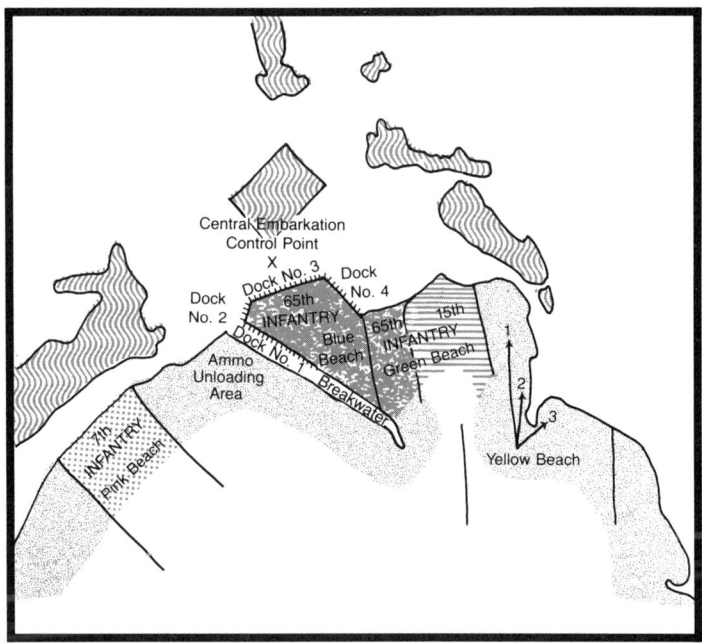

MAP No. 11 - Hungnam Harbor, showing the beaches used in the withdrawal of the 3d Infantry Divisioin.

moved to the left of the perimeter, where it supported the 7th Infantry. The 10th Field Artillery, which was the 7th Infantry's regular support battalion, moved to the middle of the perimeter in support of the 65th Infantry. Batteries A and B of the 10th Field withdrew at 7:00 A.M.; Battery C followed approximately thirty minutes later.

The 39th Field Artillery, positioned at the northeastern end of the defensive perimeter, fired in support of the 15th Infantry. It embarked at 11:00 A.M., the last artillery unit to do so.

Colonel Moore's 15th Infantry came out over Green Beach 2 and Yellow beaches 1,2, and 3. (See Map 11.) Since these beaches were located within the confines of the harbor, it was possible to bring the navy landing craft up to the pier for embarkation. The main body of the 15th Infantry embarked shortly after noon. The regimental covering force commanded by the regimental executive officer, LTC Thomas Yancey, and consisting of the regimental I & R (Intelligence & Reconnaissance) platoon, the Heavy Mortar Company, a Naval Gun Fire team and the covering force from each of the three battalions, withdrew at 1:00 P.M.

Colonel Harris's 65th Infantry, occupying the center of the line, had a tricky assignment. The withdrawal of this unit had to be closely coordinated with its two neighbors to prevent an exposed flank, yet it had to present an aggressive stance to the Chinese to keep from inviting an attack in the center of the line. Accordingly, LTC St. Clair's 1st and MAJ Allen's 3d battalions retired to Blue Beach by moving through the position occupied by LTC Dammer's 2d Battalion, whose own withdrawal was timed to be within minutes of the departure of the covering force from the 15th Infantry. By 1:30 P.M. all divisional elements were aboard landing craft and the navy underwater demolition teams began their mission of systematically destroying buildings, wharves, and railroad rolling stock with explosive charges previously placed for that purpose.[4]

At 2:40 P.M., a radio message from the command ship USS *Mount McKinley*, lying off Hungnam harbor, crackled through the airwaves advising General MacArthur's headquarters in Tokyo that all elements of X Corps had been successfully withdrawn from the beachhead.[5] In addition to 87,400 troops, the Navy brought out 86,000 civilian refugees who wished to leave (7,000 had been evacuated at Wonsan), and the following impedimenta:

17,500 vehicles plus equipment
250,000 metric tons of supplies, including
  8,635 short tons of ammunition and
29,400 drums (55 gal.) of gasoline and petroleum products.

Any hypothetical indebtedness the U.S. Navy may have had to the U.S. Army was paid off at Hungnam. The awesome destructive power of naval gunfire support and its ability to illuminate the battlefield during the long hours of darkness was, in the estimate of many, the biggest single factor that made possible the embarkation of nearly two hundred thousand troops and refugees as well as the equipment and supplies.

In the history of modern warfare only two nations have demonstrated their ability to leave a hostile shore with any semblance of order. At Dunkirk in 1940, the British, faced with a choice, wisely elected to save their men and to forgo the hope of saving their field pieces, armor, and impedimenta. At Hungnam in 1950 control of the sea and absolute dominance in the air enabled the American army to withdraw its units intact with all equipment.

In later years, Brigadier General James O. Boswell would remember the 3d Infantry Division's performance at Hungnam as "essentially an exercise in improvisation. . . . . and a great credit to the United States Army. No school in the American military establishment had a curriculum on how to evacuate a beachhead. We had been taught how to take a beach, but not how to give one up."[6]

Brigadier General Harley F. Mooney, present that day as a young lieutenant serving as aide to the assistant division commander, said, "the transformation of the 3d Infantry Division into a combat unit took place in the Hungnam perimeter. You could feel the outfit coming together. It coalesced into one helluva fine fighting outfit."[7]

At Hungnam the CCF, for the first time since their entry into the Korean war, had come face to face with a fresh infantry division whose flanks were securely anchored on the sea; one that would expend 46,000 rounds of artillery fire in a five-day period. Defensive positions had been carefully chosen and fully developed, giving the troops confidence in their ability to hold and fight in place for as long as necessary. Here the Chinese would have to fight America's kind of war, a war of massed firepower supported by air and naval forces.

Years later we were able to learn much of what happened "on the other side of the hill." Frostbite and hypothermia cost the CCF close to twenty percent of its unit strength and had thus been impartial to friend and foe alike in their diminishing the foot soldier's effectiveness. We found that prolonged exposure to subzero weather had taken its toll on the hardy Chinese soldier (who had neither gloves nor socks) just as it had on the Americans; and that tetanus, caused by improper care of wounds, was also a factor. And last, but by no means least, we learned of the price paid by the CCF armies, who were gutted by the 1st Marine Division in its epic fighting withdrawal from the Chosin Reservoir to Chinhung-ni, where it entered the 3d Infantry Division defensive perimeter.[8]

To those who lived through the ordeal with its numbing cold, windswept ridges, lack of food and sleep and, above all, the constant specter of death or captivity, the Hungnam evacuation was, indeed, a miracle of the first magnitude.

Notes

1. Diary of LTG Edward M. Almond, part of the Edward M. Almond Papers, U.S. Army Center for Military History, Carlisle Barracks, PA.

2. Author interview, BG James O. Boswell, USA (Ret.), June 3, 1989. General Boswell, executive officer of the 7th Infantry

at the time of the Hungnam operation, witnessed the accident. He was called upon to testify at a Naval Board of Inquiry.

3. The Command Reports for December 1950 from the 3d Inf Div, 7th, 15th, and 65th Infantry regiments were used as reference in determining the sequence of troop movements. On file at the U.S. Army Center for Military History, Carlisle Barracks, PA. Copies are in the author's possession.

4. There is some ambiguity in the official records as to which regiment's rearguard was, in fact, last off the beach. The Command Report for the 3d Infantry Division (December 1950) states, "the covering forces of the regiments were taken off the beach in LVTs [landing craft]; 7th Infantry cleared the beach at 1230 hours; 65th Infantry cleared at 1237 hours; 15th Infantry cleared at 1400 hours."

The Command Report for the 7th Infantry states, "all equipment evacuated by 1300 hours. The regimental commander boarded an Amtrak [amphibious tractor] at 1310 hours and officially closed Pink Beach over which the regiment had outloaded." The Command Report for the 15th Infantry states, "shortly after noon all of the main body loaded, leaving the covering force. The enemy made a small, unsuccessful attack against the roadblock area. The covering force was successfully withdrawn and loaded [aboard ship] by mid-afternoon." The Command Report for the 65th Infantry states, "2d Bn was the last to withdraw and the last group from this Bn to withdraw was a small strong point of riflemen and MGs [machine guns] on a small hill close to the beach line. The beach was cleared at 1245 hours on 24 December 1950."

BG W. W. Harris, who commanded the 65th Infantry at Hungnam, states in his book that his diary entry recorded, "my small command group loaded on last LCT with elements of the 2d Battalion at 1430 hours on 24 December 1950. So far as I know, we were the last to leave the area." (See W. W. Harris, *Puerto Rico's Fighting 65th Infantry*, p. 130.)

Every unit clamors for "bragging rights" as the first to fight and last to leave. At Hungnam, the time interval between departures of the rearguard from any two of these infantry regiments was so short as to be insignificant.

5. The message was relayed from Tokyo to Washington where President Truman was quoted as saying, "that's the best Christmas present I ever had."

6. Boswell, interview.

7. Author interview, BG Harley F. Mooney, USA (Ret.), July 26, 1989.

8. CCF losses, both battle and nonbattle, exceeded 40,000. Some units in the CCF IX Army Group were so badly mauled in their attacks on the marine division that they were out of action for three months. Others never again appeared in the enemy's order of battle.

RETROSPECT

The manner in which General Soule handled his 3d Infantry Division, once it had been consolidated in early December and deployed as a division, was a textbook example of a fighting withdrawal. Forty years after the event, it is impossible to say with any degree of certainty in which headquarters the evacuation plan for Hungnam originated.

Under ordinary circumstances the senior commander would be the one to designate the time and place of the evacuation based on logistical as well as tactical considerations. Having displayed on numerous occasions hyperactive interest in detail, it is entirely possible, indeed likely, that General Almond and his X Corps staff conceived the Hungnam operation.

But if General Almond knew planning, General Soule knew his Chinese adversary. It is more likely that the concept of phase lines, and particularly the withdrawal from those phase lines *in anticipation* of the Chinese attacks, was the product of General Soule and his 3d Division staff.[1]

The Chinese could do wondrous things on the battlefield but sustained attack and the ability to adjust to fluid conditions on short notice were not their strong suits. The CCF, lacking what modern armies would call a "logistical tail," required frequent pauses for reorganization and replenishment of supplies after each short burst of offensive operations.

General Soule was an astute observer of the Chinese Communists during his long years of service in that country. He understood the Chinese mentality; he studied their tactical concepts and knew their capabilities as well as anyone in the U.S. Army in 1950. It can be said that at Hungnam "the mission had found the man."

It is the aim of every historian to conduct his study of a military campaign in a manner that gives consideration to all aspects of the battle. It must be a fair and evenhanded approach that includes an analysis of the three Ts (tactics, terrain, and troops) in order to adjudge the mission a success or failure. The most challenging part of the task is attempting to understand the mind-set of the battlefield commander; to look over his shoulder, as it were, and see the battle as he must have seen it unfolding before him. And so an assessment of the Hungnam campaign begins by considering the performance of Lieutenant General Song Shi-lun, the commander of the Chinese IX Army Group in northeast Korea.

This forty-three-year-old native of Hunan province was a graduate of Whampoa Military Academy and a veteran of the Long March. He came to Korea with a record of distinguished military service.

Was General Song's decision to strike when and where he did a wise one? Did he deploy his troops in a manner that maximized their effectiveness?

Did he make the terrain his ally, and did he have a reasonable chance for success? And, finally, was he successful?

The timing of his attack on both the 1st Marine and 7th Infantry divisions was excellent, particularly since he caught both units in motion, i.e., in the midst of preparations for launching an offensive strike of their own. Most important, he caught both divisions with their integral units widely separated in accordance with the tactical plan of General Almond, the X Corps commander.

It was only through the stubbornness of General O. P. Smith that the 1st Marine Division was not nearly as dispersed as General Almond had desired. This was a fortuitous (perhaps *the* fortuitous) development, since it was the marine division that the CCF commander had to destroy in detail in order for the rest of his tactical plan to succeed.

Had he bypassed the marine division at Yudam-ni and made his main effort farther south at Sachang-ni or Huksu-ri (roughly forty air miles south of Yudam-ni), his chances of success would have been much greater. Whereas at Yudam-ni he faced two marine regiments with supporting artillery and armor nearby, at Sachang-ni he would have faced a single battalion of infantry, new to combat, in terrain that offered limited opportunity for the American army to use its mobility and firepower. The 1/7th Infantry at Sachang-ni was "out on a string," about forty miles from supporting units. With its CP more than eighty miles away and its organic units spread all over the landscape, the 3d Infantry Division would have been hard pressed to prevent General Song from gaining a position that would have been fatal to the marine division.[2] A victory at Sachang-ni would have placed the CCF IX Army Group about eight miles closer to the port at Hungnam than the marine division still at Yudam-ni, and in terrain better suited for the rapid deployment of light infantry. By making his main thrust against the division best prepared to resist attack in that forbidding terrain, General Song sustained troop losses that made it impossible for his army to prevail. If it was the mission of IX Army Group to evict the U.S. X Corps from North Korea, we must judge its efforts as successful. If, however, it was General Song's intent to destroy this body of troops or render it ineffective in future engagements, then his efforts ended in abject failure.

Given the state of anxiety among political and military leaders in Washington at the time, it is not unreasonable to suggest that had General Song successfully destroyed X Corps, the loss of such a significant number of troops might well have forced the United Nations (more specifically, the United States) to withdraw its entire force from the Korean peninsula and to abandon South Korea to its fate.

We now cross the front line and pose the same set of questions regarding General Almond's performance that applied to General Song.

General Almond was, to a large extent, the victim of General MacArthur's decision in November 1950 to continue offensive operations. Ironically, as we shall see shortly, he was also the cause of this questionable course of action. Eighth Army and X Corps were advancing on parallel but widely separated fronts. They were moving into rugged, mountainous country where the roadnet was limited and the opportunity for lateral movement of troops was virtually nonexistent. The terrain would be an enemy, not an ally.

Generals Walker and Almond were mounting campaigns in the most abominable weather imaginable (another enemy), and they were doing so with troops that had been "fought out" after long and arduous campaigning. Because the enemy appeared beaten, units were strung out over distances much greater than normal. The troops, particularly in X Corps, were deployed more in the manner of a quail hunt than a military campaign.

Several military historians suggest that the seeds for defeat in North Korea in December 1950 were sown in the daring success at Inchon in September. Despite physical impediments, unfavorable tides, and well reasoned objections by naval and Marine Corps personnel versed in amphibious warfare, General MacArthur had rolled the dice and won. This triumph in the face of overwhelming odds made it infinitely more difficult for his staff to take a cautious position when it became common knowledge that the Chinese colossus had come to the aid of North Korea.

Caution is to be equated with neither cowardice nor timidity. It takes a certain amount of moral courage to exercise caution on the battlefield, yet it often saves lives.

Unfortunately, General Almond, the commander on the spot, was a stranger to caution. One of his own staff members said, "when it paid to be aggressive, Ned was aggressive; and when it paid to be cautious, Ned was aggressive."[3]

A hard-driving soldier, intensely loyal and inclined to perfectionism, General Almond's personal courage and ardor for battle were beyond question. However, his concept of the role of a corps commander was not the traditional one. Impetuous and impatient, he fell into the practice of issuing orders directly to regimental commanders without observing the courtesy of advising their division commanders. This resulted in a perceptible coolness between himself and Generals Soule (3d Division), Barr (7th Division) and Smith (1st Marine Division).[4]

Colonel John S. Guthrie, when promoted to X Corps chief of staff shortly after the Hungnam operation, found the usual "good guy-bad guy" roles reversed and he spent much of his time smoothing ruffled feathers caused by the corps commander's abrasiveness.[5]

General Almond's brusque personality did nothing to inspire confidence in junior officers, and his seeming unwillingness to acknowledge the organizational differences between marine and army divisions combined to end whatever hope there might have been that he could work with the equally capable (and equally strong-willed) marine General O. P. Smith with any degree of mutual trust and respect. [6]

There were many references to "Ned the Anointed" because of the obvious favoritism he enjoyed in Tokyo. Some even suspected the underlying reason for the helter-skelter advance of X Corps to the Yalu River was to earn a third star for

Retrospect   107

the corps commander. Indeed, the campaign was known covertly as "Operation Third Star" behind Almond's back.[7]

By temperament and training General Almond was inclined to exert every effort to ensure the execution of General MacArthur's orders to continue the advance to the Yalu. And yet his firsthand knowledge of the tactical situation, and particularly his personal interrogation of several Chinese prisoners, must have told him those orders were no longer viable.[8]

General Almond's opportunity to do a noble service for his commander came at a meeting in Tokyo in the late evening of November 28, 1950, a meeting to which General Walker had also been invited. At this meeting, General MacArthur solicited the opinions of his two field commanders as to a future course of action. General Walker, ever the realist, assured General MacArthur that he could hold Pyongyang, situated at the narrow waist of the peninsula, and stated his intention to establish a *defensive* position north and east of that city. When it was time for General Almond to speak, he euphorically stated his intention to continue *offensive* operations with an attack by the 1st Marine and 7th Infantry divisions in a direction north and west of the Chosin Reservoir. Obviously, these two commanders were not participating in the same war.[9]

It would have been impossible for one of the field commanders to adopt a course of action that would contravene the operational plans of the other. Historian Clay Blair notes General MacArthur's steadily diminishing confidence in General Walker which was due, perhaps in large measure, to General Almond.[10] If there was one man in uniform in the Far East who could have dissuaded General MacArthur from continuing offensive operations in November 1950, Ned Almond was that man. Instead, he chose to tell General MacArthur what he (MacArthur) wanted to hear, not what he should have heard. General Almond thus became the victim of his own bad advice.

Admittedly, hindsight is always blessed with twenty-twenty vision. Events are seen more clearly than would ever be possible during the actual fighting. Hazards are recognized, opportunities grasped, and decisions made in a calm, objective manner not even remotely resembling the heat of battle.

It was not the author's intent for this narrative to become a definitive biography of General Almond, nor should it be considered as such. However, his personality had such a profound effect on the tactical operations of X Corps and his relationship with his subordinate commanders that it greatly influenced the outcome of events in the military campaign in northeast Korea.

Perhaps General Almond was given a mission that no man could fulfill. But to the extent that his remarks of November 28 to the men of Task Force Faith reflected his honest appraisal of the situation in northeast Korea, the corps commander must bear responsibility for the subsequent losses in men and matériel incurred in pursuit of an unrealistic and unattainable goal.[11]

And so ended the campaign in northeast Korea. General Walker's untimely death in a truck-jeep accident on December 23 brought General Matthew B. Ridgway to Korea, a man who could lead an army, fight an army, inspire an army. X Corps became an integral part of Eighth Army, as it should have been all along; and the fighting continued until the butcher's bill was more than even China, with her seemingly limitless human resources, cared to pay.

Notes

1. See Appleman, *Escaping the Trap*, p. 322.
2. When the CCF offensive began on November 27, the 3d Infantry Division CP was still in Wonsan. When 1/7th Infantry relieved the 26th ROK Regiment at Sachang-ni, the 7th Infantry's other two battalions were at Kogae-dong, roughly thirty-eight miles southeast of Sachang-ni. The 65th RCT was at Yonghung, twenty-five miles south of Chigyong with its assigned mission of moving in a westward direction toward Tongyang. See Maps 5 and 6.

If the CCF had been able to defeat the 7th Infantry in detail, the road junction at Chigyong, fifty-five miles southeast of Sachang-ni and just eight miles south of Hamhung, would have become the critical point of tactical operations for any elements of the 3d Infantry Division attempting to fight their way north.

3. Letter to author, GEN Frank T. Mildren, USA (Ret.), dated January 22, 1989.
4. Following the Hungnam operation, many staff officers in the 3d Infantry and 1st Marine divisions were pleased when these two excellent fighting units were transferred to another corps in Eighth Army.
5. Letter to author, MG John S. Guthrie, USA (Ret.), dated July 14, 1988.

6. Author interview, BG Harley F. Mooney, USA (Ret.), July 26, 1989.

7. General Almond was promoted to lieutenant general on February 15, 1951.

8. A hint of caution, evidently resulting from his interrogation of CCF prisoners on October 30, was evident in General Almond's pronouncements for a few days; however, with the disappearance of the Chinese in the first week of November, he quickly reverted to his customary mind-set.

9. See Appleman, *Escaping the Trap*, pp. 119–21, 125.

10. See Blair, *The Forgotten War*, pp. 36 and 187.

11. "The enemy who is delaying you for the moment is nothing more than remnants of Chinese divisions fleeing north. We're still attacking and going all the way to the Yalu. Don't let a bunch of Chinese laundrymen stop you."

At the time General Almond delivered this comment to the doomed men of the 31st Infantry's Task Force Faith just east of the Chosin Reservoir, about 60,000 "laundrymen" were preparing to rip into his corps. Many of them were less than five miles from where he stood; and they were heading south, not north. Another 60,000 were moving into positions from which to block all avenues of escape for the exposed forces of X Corps which were deployed over an area of three hundred square miles.

Appendix A

Strength Figures for the 3d Infantry Division on Selected Dates

Table A.1
Third Infantry Division and Organic Units Actual Strength Figures—August 23, 1950

	Authorized			Actual		
	Officer	Warrant Officer	Enlisted Men	Officer	Warrant Officer	Enlisted Men
Division Headquarters	54	08	141	64	06	168
Hq Co, 3d Infantry Div	13	00	176	10	02	124
3d Division Band	00	02	070	00	02	050
3d Medical Battalion	46	02	293	36	00	152
3d Military Police Co.	07	00	180	06	00	119
703d Ordnance Maint. Co.	15	04	302	n.a.	n.a.	n.a.
3d Quartermaster Co.	12	00	248	09	00	177
3d Reconnaissance Co.	06	00	164	07	01	081
3d Replacement Co.	06	01	034	n.a.	n.a.	n.a.
3d Signal Co.	12	03	354	14	01	208
7th Infantry						
Hq & Hq Co.	21	01	263	19	02	114
Service Co.	08	01	175	06	04	130
Hvy Mortar Co.	06	00	084	05	01	041
Heavy Tank Co.	06	00	142	05	02	116
Medical Co.	13	00	201	07	00	105
Hq & Hq Co, 1st Bn	11	00	108	09	01	042
Company A	06	00	205	05	01	034
Company B	06	00	205	04	01	100
Company C	06	00	205	04	01	033
Company D	05	00	160	04	01	043
Hq & Hq Co, 2nd Bn	11	00	108	09	01	037

Strength Figures for the 3d Infantry Division

	Authorized			Actual		
	Officer	Warrant Officer	Enlisted Men	Officer	Warrant Officer	Enlisted Men
Company E	06	00	205	05	01	024
Company F	06	00	205	04	01	025
Company G	06	00	205	04	01	021
Company H	05	00	160	04	01	024
Hq & Hq Co, 3rd Bn	11	00	108	10	01	046
Company I	06	00	205	03	01	032
Company K	06	00	205	04	01	031
Company L	06	00	205	05	01	035
Company M	05	00	160	05	01	035
15th Infantry						
Hq & Hq Co.	21	01	263	26	03	172
Service Co.	08	01	175	08	03	163
Hvy Mortar Co.	06	00	084	06	01	074
Heavy Tank Co.	06	00	142	06	01	130
Medical Co.	13	00	201	n.a.	n.a.	n.a.
Hq & Hq Co, 1st Bn	11	00	108	22	01	073
Company A	06	00	205	06	01	080
Company B	06	00	205	04	01	062
Company C	06	00	205	06	01	063
Company D	05	00	160	05	01	060
Hq & Hq Co, 2nd Bn	11	00	108	21	01	090
Company E	06	00	205	04	01	064
Company F	06	00	205	07	01	065
Company G	06	00	205	05	01	084
Company H	05	00	160	05	01	072
Hq & Hq Co, 3rd Bn	11	00	108	25	01	073
Company I	06	00	205	03	01	093
Company K	06	00	205	07	01	090
Company L	06	00	205	03	01	097
Company M	05	00	160	09	01	095
65th Infantry						
Hq & Hq Co.	21	01	263	23	08	223
Service Co.	08	01	175	05	01	086

APPENDIX A

	Authorized			Actual		
	Officer	Warrant Officer	Enlisted Men	Officer	Warrant Officer	Enlisted Men
Hvy Mortar Co.	06	00	084	06	00	129
Heavy Tank Co.	06	00	142	n.a.	n.a.	n.a.
Medical Co.	13	00	201	09	00	116
Hq & Hq Co, 1st Bn	11	00	108	10	00	091
Company A	06	00	205	06	01	143
Company B	06	00	205	05	00	149
Company C	06	00	205	05	01	188
Company D	05	00	160	06	00	110
Hq & Hq Co, 2nd Bn	11	00	108	11	03	101
Company E	06	00	205	06	00	148
Company F	06	00	205	06	01	134
Company G	06	00	205	06	00	146
Company H	05	00	160	05	00	108
Hq & Hq Co, 3rd Bn	11	00	108	20	00	168
Company I	06	00	205	06	01	124
Company K	06	00	205	06	00	130
Company L	06	00	205	06	00	122
Company M	05	00	160	05	00	144
3d Division Artillery						
Hq & Hq Btry	24	01	132	24	03	107
Medical Det.	07	00	063	04	00	007
10th Field Artillery Bn						
Hq & Hq Btry	19	01	147	21	02	099
Battery A	08	00	131	09	00	049
Battery B	08	00	131	09	01	050
Battery C	08	00	131	09	01	051
Svc Battery	03	01	081	04	02	072
39th Field Artillery Bn						
Hq & Hq Btry	19	01	147	25	02	090
Battery A	08	00	131	09	00	066
Battery B	08	00	131	11	00	071
Battery C	08	00	131	09	01	073
Svc Battery	03	01	081	03	01	059

Strength Figures for the 3d Infantry Division

	Authorized			Actual		
	Officer	Warrant Officer	Enlisted Men	Officer	Warrant Officer	Enlisted Men
58th Armored F/A Bn						
Hq & Hq Btry	19	01	147	17	01	107
Battery A	08	00	131	05	01	089
Battery B	08	00	131	05	00	081
Battery C	08	00	131	05	00	084
Svc Battery	03	01	081	05	00	071
999th Armored F/A Bn						
Hq & Hq Btry	17	01	124	18	02	118
Battery A	05	00	139	07	01	133
Battery B	05	00	139	07	01	125
Battery C	05	00	139	08	01	118
Svc Battery	03	01	083	05	02	101
3d AAA AW Bn						
Hq & Hq Btry	12	02	147	12	02	121
Battery A	06	00	147	06	01	100
Battery B	06	00	147	07	01	091
Battery C	06	00	147	07	01	087
Battery D	06	00	147	06	01	090
64th Heavy Tank Bn						
Hq & Hq & Sv Co.	16	03	195	14	03	177
Company A	06	00	142	03	00	108
Company B	06	00	142	04	00	102
Company C	06	00	142	04	00	101
Medical Det.	02	00	017	01	00	014
10th Engineer (C) Bn						
Hq & Hq & Svc Co.	20	03	253	15	02	132
Company A	05	00	163	02	00	091
Company B	05	00	163	04	00	045
Company C	05	00	163	04	01	057
Company D	05	00	163	05	00	047
Medical Det.	02	00	022	02	00	005

Source: "Present for Duty" column, Morning Report WD AGO Form 1, for date indicated. On file at Military Personnel Records Center, St. Louis, MO.

APPENDIX A   115

Table A.2
THIRD INFANTRY DIVISION AND ORGANIC UNITS
ACTUAL STRENGTH FIGURES—NOVEMBER 23, 1950

	Authorized			Actual		
	Officer	Warrant Officer	Enlisted Men	Officer	Warrant Officer	Enlisted Men
Division Headquarters	54	08	141	89	05	215
Hq Co, 3d Infantry Div	13	00	176	15	03	165
3d Division Band	00	02	070	00	02	065
3d Medical Batalion	46	02	293	30	02	281
3d Military Police Co.	07	00	180	10	00	155
703d Ordnance Maint. Co.	15	04	302	n.a.	n.a.	n.a.
3d Quartermaster Co.	12	00	248	12	00	218
3d Reconnaissance Co.	06	00	164	06	01	133
3d Replacement Co.	06	01	034	06	00	034
3d Signal Co.	12	03	354	14	02	274
7th Infantry						
Hq & Hq Co.	21	01	263	28	02	222
Service Co.	08	01	175	08	05	140
Hvy Mortar Co.	06	00	084	06	00	140
Heavy Tank Co.	06	00	142	06	01	126
Medical Co.	13	00	201	14	00	180
Hq & Hq Co, 1st Bn	11	00	108	13	01	100
Company A	06	00	205	06	01	135
Company B	06	00	205	06	01	131
Company C	06	00	205	06	01	136
Company D	05	00	160	05	01	141
Hq & Hq Co, 2nd Bn	11	00	108	12	01	099
Company E	06	00	205	06	00	133
Company F	06	00	205	06	01	139
Company G	06	00	205	06	01	132
Company H	05	00	160	06	00	138
Hq & Hq Co, 3rd Bn	11	00	108	13	01	104
Company I	06	00	205	06	01	133
Company K	06	00	205	06	01	148
Company L	06	00	205	05	01	128
Company M	05	00	160	05	00	147

Strength Figures for the 3d Infantry Division

	Authorized			Actual		
	Officer	Warrant Officer	Enlisted Men	Officer	Warrant Officer	Enlisted Men
15th Infantry						
Hq & Hq Co.	21	01	263	30	03	211
Service Co.	08	01	175	08	06	139
Hvy Mortar Co.	06	00	084	03	01	069
Heavy Tank Co.	06	00	142	06	01	099
Medical Co.	13	00	201	09	00	084
Hq & Hq Co, 1st Bn	11	00	108	17	01	181
Company A	06	00	205	06	00	124
Company B	06	00	205	04	01	111
Company C	06	00	205	06	01	124
Company D	05	00	160	04	01	086
Hq & Hq Co, 2nd Bn	11	00	108	16	00	157
Company E	06	00	205	06	01	116
Company F	06	00	205	05	01	115
Company G	06	00	205	06	01	124
Company H	05	00	160	04	01	086
Hq & Hq Co, 3rd Bn	11	00	108	14	01	171
Company I	06	00	205	07	00	195
Company K	06	00	205	06	01	192
Company L	06	00	205	06	00	190
Company M	05	00	160	04	01	148
65th Infantry						
Hq & Hq Co.	21	01	263	22	03	317
Service Co.	08	01	175	10	05	255
Hvy Mortar Co.	06	00	084	04	01	185
Heavy Tank Co.	06	00	142	05	00	076
Medical Co.	13	00	201	12	00	217
Hq & Hq Co, 1st Bn	11	00	108	12	00	125
Company A	06	00	205	05	01	204
Company B	06	00	205	06	01	200
Company C	06	00	205	06	01	195
Company D	05	00	160	05	01	170
Hq & Hq Co, 2nd Bn	11	00	108	11	01	111

Appendix A

	Authorized			Actual		
	Officer	Warrant Officer	Enlisted Men	Officer	Warrant Officer	Enlisted Men
Company E	06	00	205	05	01	198
Company F	06	00	205	06	01	201
Company G	06	00	205	05	01	195
Company H	05	00	160	05	01	164
Hq & Hq Co, 3rd Bn	11	00	108	13	00	127
Company I	06	00	205	06	00	206
Company K	06	00	205	05	00	216
Company L	06	00	205	05	00	215
Company M	05	00	160	04	00	166
3d Division Artillery						
Hq & Hq Btry	24	01	132	24	03	124
Medical Det.	07	00	063	02	00	062
10th Field Artillery Bn						
Hq & Hq Btry	19	01	147	25	02	125
Battery A	08	00	131	08	01	101
Battery B	08	00	131	08	01	198
Battery C	08	00	131	08	01	102
Svc Battery	03	01	081	04	02	056
39th Field Artillery Bn						
Hq & Hq Btry	19	01	147	28	01	122
Battery A	08	00	131	08	01	096
Battery B	08	00	131	08	01	101
Battery C	08	00	131	09	01	099
Svc Battery	03	01	081	03	02	069
58th Armored F/A Bn						
Hq & Hq Btry	19	01	147	n.a.	n.a.	n.a.
Battery A	08	00	131	n.a.	n.a.	n.a.
Battery B	08	00	131	n.a.	n.a.	n.a.
Battery C	08	00	131	n.a.	n.a.	n.a.
Svc Battery	03	01	081	n.a.	n.a.	n.a.
999th Armored F/A Bn						
Hq & Hq Btry	17	01	124	23	02	132
Battery A	05	00	139	05	01	141
Battery B	05	00	139	06	01	142

Strength Figures for the 3d Infantry Division

	Authorized			Actual		
	Officer	Warrant Officer	Enlisted Men	Officer	Warrant Officer	Enlisted Men
Battery C	05	00	139	06	01	143
Svc Battery	03	01	083	05	02	099
3d AAA AW Bn						
Hq & Hq Btry	12	02	147	13	02	093
Battery A	06	00	147	06	01	104
Battery B	06	00	147	06	01	100
Battery C	06	00	147	07	01	087
Battery D	06	00	147	06	01	097
64th Heavy Tank Bn						
Hq & Hq & Svc Co.	16	03	195	18	03	190
Company A	06	00	142	07	01	139
Company B	06	00	142	08	00	138
Company C	06	00	142	08	00	138
Medical Det.	02	00	017	02	00	017
10th Engineer (C) Bn						
Hq & Hq & Svc Co.	20	03	253	18	04	225
Company A	05	00	163	04	01	125
Company B	05	00	163	04	01	107
Company C	05	00	163	04	01	061
Company D	05	00	163	04	01	123
Medical Det.	02	00	022	02	00	009

Source: "Present for Duty" column, Morning Report WD AGO Form 1, for date indicated. On file at Military Personnel Records Center, St. Louis, MO.

Table A.3
THIRD INFANTRY DIVISION AND ORGANIC UNITS
ACTUAL STRENGTH FIGURES — DECEMBER 24, 1950

	Authorized			Actual		
	Officer	Warrant Officer	Enlisted Men	Officer	Warrant Officer	Enlisted Men
Division Headquarters	54	08	141	91	05	220
Hq Co, 3d Infantry Div	13	00	176	12	03	156
3d Division Band	00	02	070	00	02	054
3d Medical Batalion	46	02	293	30	02	277
3d Military Police Co.	07	00	180	08	00	146
703d Ordnance Maint. Co.	15	04	302	n.a.	n.a.	n.a.
3d Quartermaster Co.	12	00	248	10	00	212
3d Reconnaissance Co.	06	00	164	07	01	134
3d Replacement Co.	06	01	034	05	00	033
3d Signal Co.	12	03	354	15	02	298
7th Infantry						
Hq & Hq Co.	21	01	263	25	02	218
Service Co.	08	01	175	07	05	130
Hvy Mortar Co.	06	00	084	06	01	130
Heavy Tank Co.	06	00	142	05	01	117
Medical Co.	13	00	201	14	00	157
Hq & Hq Co, 1st Bn	11	00	108	12	00	101
Company A	06	00	205	06	01	106
Company B	06	00	205	02	01	108
Company C	06	00	205	04	01	101
Company D	05	00	160	04	01	134
Hq & Hq Co, 2nd Bn	11	00	108	10	01	082
Company E	06	00	205	05	00	094
Company F	06	00	205	05	01	090
Company G	06	00	205	03	01	067
Company H	05	00	160	04	01	117
Hq & Hq Co, 3rd Bn	11	00	108	13	01	099
Company I	06	00	205	05	01	116
Company K	06	00	205	04	01	138
Company L	06	00	205	05	01	121
Company M	05	00	160	05	00	140

Strength Figures for the 3d Infantry Division

	Authorized			Actual		
	Officer	Warrant Officer	Enlisted Men	Officer	Warrant Officer	Enlisted Men
15th Infantry						
Hq & Hq Co.	21	01	263	31	03	200
Service Co.	08	01	175	08	06	133
Hvy Mortar Co.	06	00	084	02	01	062
Heavy Tank Co.	06	00	142	06	01	092
Medical Co.	13	00	201	10	00	079
Hq & Hq Co, 1st Bn	11	00	108	14	01	174
Company A	06	00	205	05	00	088
Company B	06	00	205	05	01	098
Company C	06	00	205	05	01	114
Company D	05	00	160	05	01	078
Hq & Hq Co, 2nd Bn	11	00	108	15	00	150
Company E	06	00	205	05	01	109
Company F	06	00	205	07	01	114
Company G	06	00	205	06	01	123
Company H	05	00	160	05	01	084
Hq & Hq Co, 3rd Bn	11	00	108	15	00	164
Company I	06	00	205	06	00	178
Company K	06	00	205	05	01	176
Company L	06	00	205	04	01	129
Company M	05	00	160	04	01	142
65th Infantry						
Hq & Hq Co.	21	01	263	28	03	316
Service Co.	08	01	175	09	05	246
Hvy Mortar Co.	06	00	084	04	01	185
Heavy Tank Co.	06	00	142	05	00	127
Medical Co.	13	00	201	10	00	194
Hq & Hq Co, 1st Bn	11	00	108	12	00	116
Company A	06	00	205	05	01	187
Company B	06	00	205	03	01	176
Company C	06	00	205	04	01	189
Company D	05	00	160	04	01	168

Appendix A

	Authorized			Actual		
	Officer	Warrant Officer	Enlisted Men	Officer	Warrant Officer	Enlisted Men
Hq & Hq Co, 2nd Bn	11	00	108	11	01	110
Company E	06	00	205	05	01	188
Company F	06	00	205	05	01	194
Company G	06	00	205	05	01	193
Company H	05	00	160	05	01	157
Hq & Hq Co, 3rd Bn	11	00	108	11	00	116
Company I	06	00	205	05	00	192
Company K	06	00	205	04	00	194
Company L	06	00	205	04	00	201
Company M	05	00	160	04	00	154
3d Division Artillery						
Hq & Hq Btry	24	01	132	26	03	134
Medical Det.	07	00	063	03	00	072
10th Field Artillery Bn						
Hq & Hq Btry	19	01	147	24	02	123
Battery A	08	00	131	08	01	095
Battery B	08	00	131	06	01	093
Battery C	08	00	131	07	01	097
Svc Battery	03	01	081	04	02	056
39th Field Artillery Bn						
Hq & Hq Btry	19	01	147	24	01	125
Battery A	08	00	131	08	01	100
Battery B	08	00	131	09	01	101
Battery C	08	00	131	05	01	099
Svc Battery	03	01	081	03	02	068
58th Armored F/A Bn						
Hq & Hq Btry	19	01	147	22	01	123
Battery A	08	00	131	09	00	111
Battery B	08	00	131	07	01	103
Battery C	08	00	131	07	01	110
Svc Battery	03	01	081	03	03	087

Strength Figures for the 3d Infantry Division

	Authorized			Actual		
	Officer	Warrant Officer	Enlisted Men	Officer	Warrant Officer	Enlisted Men
999th Armored F/A Bn						
Hq & Hq Btry	17	01	124	19	02	131
Battery A	05	00	139	05	01	139
Battery B	05	00	139	06	01	142
Battery C	05	00	139	05	01	137
Svc Battery	03	01	083	04	02	097
3d AAA AW Bn						
Hq & Hq Btry	12	02	147	10	02	095
Battery A	06	00	147	06	01	103
Battery B	06	00	147	06	01	091
Battery C	06	00	147	07	01	089
Battery D	06	00	147	06	01	090
64th Heavy Tank Bn						
Hq & Hq & Svc Co.	16	03	195	18	03	187
Company A	06	00	142	07	01	136
Company B	06	00	142	07	01	137
Company C	06	00	142	08	00	132
Medical Det.	02	00	017	02	00	017
10th Engineer (C) Bn						
Hq & Hq & Svc Co.	20	03	253	16	04	237
Company A	05	00	163	04	01	116
Company B	05	00	163	04	00	100
Company C	05	00	163	02	00	100
Company D	05	00	163	04	01	120
Medical Det.	02	00	022	02	00	009

Source: "Present for Duty" column, Morning Report WD AGO Form 1, for date indicated. On file at Military Personnel Records Center, St. Louis, MO.

Appendix B

A Brief History of the 3d Infantry Division

The 3d United States Infantry Division was formed at Camp Green, North Carolina, in November 1917, shortly after the United States entered World War I. Organized as a "square" division (so named because of the squared appearance of its organizational chart), its two brigades consisted of the 4th, 7th, 30th and 38th Infantry regiments.

During World War I the division engaged in combat in the Aisne, Champagne-Marne, Aisne-Marne, St. Mihiel, Meuse-Argonne, and Champagne campaigns. On July 15–17, 1918, at the approaches to the Marne River and Paris, the 3d Division stopped the German offensive cold, thus earning the name "The Rock of the Marne." Following the armistice in November 1918 and a brief tour of occupation duty in Coblenz, Germany, the division returned to the United States. In 1922 it was given a permanent assignment at Fort Lewis, Washington.

On the eve of World War II the division reorganized into a new "triangular" concept with three, rather than four, infantry regiments. The 4th and 38th Infantry regiments were reassigned to other divisions and the 15th Infantry, returning after more than twenty-six years in China, became a part of the 3d Division.

In 531 days of combat beginning in November of 1942 (more than any other U.S. infantry division), the 3d Division suffered the heaviest casualties of any American combat unit with 6,240 killed, 24,793 wounded and 3,191 missing.

Battle credits include Algeria-French Morocco, Tunisia, Sicily, Naples-Foggia, Anzio, Rome-Arno, Southern France, Rhineland, Ardennes-Alsace, and Central Europe. By V-E Day, the division had reached Salzburg, Austria. Along the way, soldiers of the 3d Division had earned thirty-nine Congressional Medals of Honor, one hundred and thirty-three Distinguished Service Crosses, and hundreds of lesser medals. One notable honoree was a young, freckle-faced Texan named Audie L. Murphy, the most decorated American soldier of the war.

On August 27, 1946, after fifteen months of occupation duty in central Europe, the 3d Division sailed from Bremerhaven, Germany, en route to its new station at Camp Campbell, Kentucky. By the end of 1946, the division comprised only a headquarters cadre of sixteen officers and twelve enlisted men.

In 1948, when the Soviet Union initiated the blockade of West Berlin, the 3d Division was returned to active status and moved to Fort Benning, Georgia, where its buildup began.

The division was still in the early phases of unit training in June 1950, when the Korean War began. Initially it was subjected to personnel levies required to fill out the understrength units sent to

Korea. Two months after hostilities began it, too, was ordered to the Far East. A brief stopover in Japan allowed time for the division to receive additional personnel and equipment and to achieve a basic level of combat proficiency.

The 3d Division landed at Wonsan, North Korea, in early November, where it was assigned to X Corps. It played an important role in the evacuation at Hungnam and in subsequent campaigns in the area of the Iron Triangle. In 750 days of combat, the division earned battle credits in following Korean campaigns:

Chinese Communist Forces (CCF) Intervention; First United Nations (UN) Counteroffensive; CCF Spring Offensive; UN Summer-Fall Offensive; Second Korean Winter; Korea, Summer-Fall 1952; Third Korean Winter; and Korea-Summer 1953.

The division returned to the United States in October 1954 and was once again stationed at Fort Benning. In April 1958, it replaced the 10th Infantry Division in Germany, where it remains today.

BIBLIOGRAPHY

1. Archival Sources

    National Archives, Suitland, MD
    a. GHQ, X Corps, Special Report on Chosin Reservoir, November 27 to December 10, 1950.
    b. X Corps War Diary/Command Report, November 1950, Record Group 407, Box 1983.

    U.S. Army Military History Institute, Carlisle Barracks, PA
    a. 3d Infantry Division, Command Reports for November and December, 1950.
    b. Papers of LTG Edward M. Almond, CG, X Corps, including letters, files and memoranda:
       Diary of LTG Edward M. Almond.
       An Oral History by CPT Thomas Fergusson.
    c. Papers of GEN Frank T. Mildren:
       An Oral History (Project 80-3) by LTC James T. Scott, (1980).
    d. Tables of Organization and Equipment quoted in the narrative.

U.S. Army Military Personnel Records Center, St. Louis, MO

Morning Reports (WD AGO Form 1) for all units organic to the 3d Infantry Division on dates shown in narrative.

U.S. Navy Historical Center, Deck Log Section, Ships Historical Branch, Washington, DC

Verification of sailing/arrival dates of USS *General W. A. Mann* (AP-112), August–September 1950.

2. Secondary Sources

Alexander, Bevin, *Korea—The First War We Lost*, New York: Hippocrene, 1986.

Appleman, Roy E., *The United States Army in the Korean War*, Volume 1, *South to the Naktong, North to the Yalu*, Washington, DC: U.S. Government Printing Office, 1960.

_____, *East of Chosin: Entrapment and Breakout in Korea*, College Station, TX: Texas A& M University Press, 1987.

_____, *Disaster in Korea: The Chinese Confront MacArthur*, College Station, TX: Texas A& M University Press, 1989.

_____, *Escaping the Trap: The U.S. Army X Corps in Northeast Korea, 1950*, College Station, TX: Texas A& M University Press, 1990.

_____, *Ridgway Duels for Korea*, College Station, TX: Texas A& M University Press, 1990.

Blair, Clay, *The Forgotten War*, New York: Times Books, 1987.

Fehrenbach, T. R., *This Kind of War*, New York: The Macmillan Company, 1963.

George, Alexander L., *The Chinese Communist Army in Action*, New York: Columbia University Press, 1967.

Goulden, Joseph C., *Korea—The Untold Story of the War*, New York: Times Books, 1982.

Gugeler, Russell A., *Combat Actions in Korea*, Washington, DC: U.S. Government Printing Office, 1954.

Hammel, Eric, *Chosin*, New York: Vanguard Press, 1981.

Harris, W. W., *Puerto Rico's Fighting 65th Infantry*, Novato, CA: Presidio Press, 1980

Hastings, Max, *The Korean War*, New York: Touchstone Books, 1988.

Heinl, Robert Debs, *Victory at High Tide*, New York: Lippincott, 1968.

Higgins, Trumbull, *Korea and the Fall of MacArthur—A Precis in Limited War*, New York: Oxford University Press, 1960.

Knox, Donald, *The Korean War: Pusan to Chosin*, San Diego: Harcourt, Brace, Jovanovich, 1985.

Leckie, Robert, *Conflict*, New York: G.P. Putnam's Sons, 1962.

MacArthur, Douglas, *Reminiscences*, New York: McGraw-Hill, 1964.

Manchester, William, *American Caesar*, Boston: Little, Brown, 1978.

Montross, Lynn and Capt. Nicholas A. Canzona, *U.S. Marine Operations in Korea*, Volume 3, *The Chosin Campaign*, Washington, DC: U.S. Government Printing Office, 1957.

Rees, David, *Korea—The Limited War*, New York: St. Martin's Press, 1964.

Ridgway, Matthew B., *The Korean War*, New York: Doubleday, 1967.

Schnabel, James F., *U.S. Army in the Korean War—Policy and Direction: The First Year*, Washington, DC: U.S. Government Printing Office, 1970.

Smith, Robert, *MacArthur in Korea*, New York: Simon & Schuster, 1982.

Spurr, Russell, *Enter the Dragon*, New York: Newmarket, 1977.

Stanton, Shelby L., *America's Tenth Legion—X Corps in Korea*, Novato, CA: Presidio Press, 1989.

Whitney, Courtney, *MacArthur: His Rendezvous with Destiny*, New York: Alfred A. Knopf, 1956.

Willoughby, Charles A. and John A. Chamberlin, *MacArthur 1941–1951*, New York: McGraw-Hill, 1954.

INDEX

Air Force, U.S., 46, 49, 68, 90, 96
Allen, MAJ Edward G. ("Jerry"), 26, 94
Almond, MG Edward M. ("Ned"), 12, 13, 85
 concept of corps commander's role, 106
 deployment of troops, 101, 103, 105–06
 junior officers lack confidence in, 106
 personality of, 39, 105–06
 relationship with division commanders, 67, 106, 108
 relationship with General MacArthur, 106–08
 visits Hungnam beachhead, 91
American soldier, 5
 effects of CCF whistles and bugles on, 53
 obsolete equipment, 7, 15
 piecemeal commitment to combat, 15
 training and loss of combat skills, 5, 7, 15
Anbyon, North Korea, 43, 45, 61
Armament, Infantry battalion, 8 n.1
Armies, Chinese Communist
 20th Army, 56, 87 n.4
 26th Army, 87 n.4
 27th Army, 87 n.4
 38th Army, 54
 39th Army, 54
 40th Army, 54
 42nd Army, 54–57
 50th Army, 54
 66th Army, 54
Armies, U. S.
 Eighth United States (EUSAK), 7, 13, 15, 17, 39, 45–46, 49, 54, 56, 62, 104, 109
Army Groups, Chinese Communist
 IX Army Group, 57, 102, 104
 XIII Army Group, 54

Barr, MG David G., 106
Bartlett, LTC William G., Jr., 27
Battalions, ROK
 1st ROK Marine Corps, 13, 63, 66, 76, 81
 2/10th ROK Regiment, 45
 3d ROK Marine Corps, 13, 39–40, 42–43, 65–66
 5th ROK Marine Corps, 39–40, 43
Battalions, U.S.
 1/1st Marines, 70
 1/7th Infantry, 29, 35, 46–47, 49, 65, 81, 103
 1/15th Infantry, 29, 41–43, 79, 82, 85-86

1/65th Infantry, 30, 45, 65, 80, 83, 89–90, 94
2/7th Infantry, 29, 47, 49, 65–66, 81–82, 86
2/15th Infantry, 29, 63, 79, 90
2/65th Infantry 29, 66, 89, 94
3/7th Infantry, 29, 47, 63, 66, 68, 76, 83
3/15th Infantry, 30, 66, 79, 90
3/32d Infantry, 83
3/65th Infantry, 30, 79, 82–83, 86, 89–90, 94
3d AAA AW, 27, 40, 66, 68, 79, 86, 92
3d Medical, 40
9th Field Artillery, 16
10th Engineer (C), 83
10th Field Artillery, 25, 39, 79, 94
15th AAA AW, 86
31st Field Artillery, 70
39th Field Artillery, 26, 40, 43, 79, 90, 94
41st Field Artillery, 16
52d Transportation Truck, 68
58th Armored Field Artillery, 16, 26, 40, 79, 92
64th Heavy Tank, 16, 27, 40, 62, 66, 77, 83, 85
73d Heavy Tank, 16
73d Engineer (C), 68
92d Armored Field Artillery, 68
999th Armored Field Artillery, 26, 70, 79
Batteries
　A, 3d AAA AW Battalion, 40
　A, 10th Field Artillery, 94
　A, 96th Field Artillery, 41
　B, 10th Field Artillery, 94
　C, 10th Field Artillery, 94
　Hq & Hq Battery, 3d AAA AW Battalion, 68
Bayne, LTC Joseph M., 24
Besson, LTC Robert, 25
Blanchard, LTC Robert M., 26, 41–42, 79

Blue Beach, 94
Boswell, LTC James O., 24, 96
Broyles, LTC Ned B., 23

Camp Chickamauga, Japan, 21
Camp Hancock, GA, 21
Chiang Kai-shek, 51–52
Chigyong, North Korea, 11, 41, 61–63, 65
Childs, LTC George W., 26
Chinese (CCF) soldier
　casualties, 97, 99 n.8
　courage and morale, 53
　diversity of weaponry, 53–54
　General Stilwell's opinion of, 59
　hypothermia and winter clothing, 52, 95, 97
　kindness to enemy wounded, 52
　limited artillery and air support, 27, 58
　night fighting tactics, 58–59
　physical characteristics, 52
　physical/mental state at Hungnam, 90
　primitive signal equipment, 53
　removal of dead/wounded from battlefield, 52
　training and combat experience, 51–52, 58, 82
　wearing U.S. uniforms, 79
Chinhung-ni, North Korea, 12, 25, 58, 68, 70–71, 97
Chosin (Changjin) Reservoir, 12, 55, 58, 67, 97, 107
Chowon, North Korea, 63
Chung-dong, North Korea, 63
Chunking, China, 22
Communications, U.S.
　personnel and equipment, 35–36, 37 n.3
　effects of terrain and weather, 33–34
Companies, U.S.
　3d Military Police, 77

Index

3d Reconnaissance, 43, 63, 66, 68, 77, 92
3d Signal, 40–41, 66, 68
A, 10th Engineer (C) Bn, 40
A, 64th Heavy Tank Bn, 85
A, 73d Engineer (C) Bn, 68
B, 7th Infantry, 77, 79, 81
B, 10th Engineer (C) Bn, 40
B, 64th Heavy Tank Bn, 40, 66, 85, 92
B, 65th Infantry, 45–46, 80
C, 7th Infantry, 47, 49, 81
C, 10th Engineer (C) Bn, 40
C, 64th Heavy Tank Bn, 40, 85
C, 65th Infantry, 80
D, 10th Engineer (C) Bn, 72 n.15, 73 n.15
E, 15th Infantry, 86
F, 7th Infantry, 65, 79
F, 15th Infantry, 89
G, 7th Infantry, 65, 81
G, 15th Infantry, 86
G, 65th Infantry, 70
I, 15th Infantry, 86
I, 65th Infantry, 80
L, 7th Infantry, 81
L, 15th Infantry, 90
Hvy Mortar Co, 15th Infantry, 66, 94
Hvy Tank Co, 15th Infantry, 43, 90
Corps
 ROK II, 54
 U.S. I, 13
 U.S. IX, 13
 U.S. X, 11–13, 17–18, 25, 39, 45–47, 49, 55, 61–63, 66, 81, 85, 95, 101, 103–06, 108–09
Crizer, 1LT Pat W., 28

Dammer, LTC Herman W., 26, 94
Daniel, CPT John T., 24
Dawalt, LTC Kenneth F., 27, 70
Detachments
 3d CIC, 77

Divisions, CCF
 58th, 57
 60th, 58
 79th, 58
 80th, 58
 89th, 56
 124th, 55
 126th, 55
Divisions, NKPA
 1st, 87 n.4
 3d, 87 n.4
Divisions, ROK
 Capital, 19
 1st, 18
 3d, 19, 55
 6th, 54
 7th, 18
Divisions, U.S.
 1st Cavalry, 7, 55
 1st Infantry, 5
 1st Marine, 12, 18, 39, 46, 56, 57, 66–68, 71, 72 n.11, 73 n.16, 103, 106–07
 2d Armored, 16, 27
 2d Infantry, 15, 17
 3d Infantry, 11–12, 16–17, 21–22, 26, 28, 39, 47, 49, 61–63, 65, 67–68, 70–71, 76–77, 81–83, 86 87, 91, 96–97, 101, 103, 106
 7th Infantry, 7, 12, 18, 55, 58, 63, 65, 67, 71, 75, 81–83, 85–87, 103, 106–07
 11th Airborne, 22
 24th Infantry, 7
 25th Infantry, 7
 82d Airborne, 5, 16
Doe, LTC Robert E., 24
Downing, LTC Walter A., 25
Dunkirk, evacuation at, 96

Farrell, LTC Edward L., Jr., 26, 79
FECOM (Far East Command), 13
Field Army
 CCF 3d, 56

Fort Benning, GA, 16, 22, 27
Fort Bragg, NC, 5
Fort Devens, MA, 5, 36
Fort Douglas, UT, 22
Fort Hood, TX, 16, 27
Fort Leavenworth, KS, 22
Fort Lewis, WA, 15, 21
Fort McKinley, P.I., 21
Friend, MAJ James W., 23
Fusen Reservoir, 55

Gibson, LTC Erwin D., 23
Green Beach Two, 94
Gross, LTC Leslie M., 24
Gunfire, AAA, Artillery, Naval, 90
Guthrie, COL John S., 24, 92, 106

Hadongsan-ni, North Korea, 41
Hagaru-ri, North Korea, 57, 67
Hamhung, North Korea, 9, 11–12, 41, 46–47, 61–63, 65–68, 71, 75–77, 79, 82–83
Hasa-ri, North Korea, 43
Harris, COL William W., 26, 45, 94
Heinrich, LTC Charles T., 25
Hill, LTC Clifford B., 24
Hinkley, LTC Olin T., 24
Hoskot, LTC Nathaniel R., 23, 82
Hoeyang, North Korea, 61
Hongwon, North Korea, 11
Huksu-ri, North Korea, 11, 46, 62–63, 65–66, 103
Hungnam, North Korea, 11, 40–41, 66, 71, 75–76, 79, 82, 89, 91, 95–97, 101–02, 104
Huston, LTC Milburn N. ("Mel"), 26

Imjin River, 9
Inchon, Korea, 13, 18, 39, 105
Infantry division components, 1, 3–4
Inhung, North Korea, 62–63, 65

Jongiwon-ni, North Korea, 43

Kail, LTC Samuel G., 25, 81
Kogae-dong, North Korea, 41, 47
Koto-ri, North Korea, 67–68, 70
Kowon, North Korea, 11, 40, 46, 62
Kulbes, CPT Phillips A., 72 n.15
Kwangchon, North Korea, 45, 65

Laramie, WY, 21
Levy, LTC Julius, 24
Line Able, 76, 81–83, 86, 89
Line Charlie, 71, 75–76, 80–81
Line Fox, 76, 82–83, 86, 89–90, 92
Line George, 76, 81–82, 83
Line King, 76, 80–83
Line Mike, 76, 82–83
Line Peter, 76, 81, 83, 89
Line Queen, 76, 81, 83
Line Tare, 76, 81
Logan County, WV, 12

MacArthur, GEN Douglas, 13, 16, 95, 104–05
  decision to attack at Inchon, 17
  evaluation of CCF threat to intervene, 19
  relationship with Generals Almond and Walker, 107–08
Majon-dong, North Korea, 62–63, 68, 70–71, 75
Majon-ni, North Korea, 9, 40–43, 61
Malone, LTC Robert R., 24
Manila, liberation of, 22
Manpojin, North Korea, 54
Mao Tse-tung, 51
McDowell County, WV, 12
Mead, BG Armistead D., 23–24, 62, 68
Midon-ni, North Korea, 46, 62
Mingo County, WV, 12

Mitchell, MAJ George, 25
Mooney, 1LT Harley F., Jr., 24, 68, 96
Moore, COL Dennis M. ("Dinty"), 25, 94

Naktong River, 17
Navy, U.S., 90, 92, 95
 illumination of battlefield, 80, 90
Neely, LTC Robert B., 26
Newbury, LTC Alvin L., 27
Newman, COL Oliver P., 23
North Korea, People's Republic of, 15, 95
 road net and terrain, 9, 11–12
North Korean People's Army, 15, 53, 67

Ordnance Bomb Disposal Unit, 68
O'Neill, LTC Thomas A., 25
Oro-ri, North Korea, 12, 63, 66, 75, 77, 80

Paek-san, North Korea, 45, 61
Partridge, LTC Stanley H., 24
Peck, LTC Allen L., 26, 79
Peking, China, 22
Piaseczny, MAJ Joseph J., 35, 37
Pink Beach, 92
Pungson-ni, North Korea, 65
Pukchin, North Korea, 54
Pusan, Korea, 9, 15, 18
Pyongyang, North Korea, 9, 18, 107

Regiments, CCF
 370th, 55
Regiments, ROK
 2d, 54
 10th, 45
 26th, 13, 39, 41, 45–47, 55
Regiments, U.S.
 7th Infantry, 22, 24–25, 27–28, 39, 47, 57, 62–63, 65–66, 75, 77, 79, 81–83, 85–86, 89, 92, 94
 7th Marines, 55
 8th Cavalry, 54–55
 15th Infantry, 22, 25–28, 40, 45, 62, 79, 86, 89, 92, 94–95
 16th Infantry, 22
 17th Infantry, 83, 86
 29th Infantry, 22
 30th Infantry, 16, 26
 31st Infantry, 21, 58, 67
 32d Infantry, 66, 86
 33d Infantry, 26
 38th Infantry, 22
 65th Infantry, 12, 16, 26, 39–40, 45–47, 62, 66, 68, 71, 75, 77, 79, 81, 83, 86, 92, 94
 187th Airborne (RCT), 3
 188th Glider Infantry, 22
Ridgway, GEN Matthew B., 23, 109
Rieger, LTC Nathaniel B., 24
Rogers, LTC James E., 24
ROK (Republic of Korea) soldier, 15, 28
 ability to identify Chinese, 29
 assignment as translators, 29
 feeding and sanitation, 28–29
 unreliability in combat, 52 54
Rush, LTC Peter S., 24
Russian T-34 tank, 15

Sachang-ni, North Korea, 11, 46–47, 56, 62, 65, 103–04
St. Clair, LTC Howard B. ("Saint"), 26, 45, 94
Seoul, Korea, 9, 15, 18, 54
Shugg, BG Roland P., 23
Singosan, North Korea, 43, 45, 61
Sinhung, North Korea, 61
Sinhung-ni, North Korea, 62, 77
Sinuiju, North Korea, 54
Smith, MG Oliver P., USMC, 103, 106
Song, General Shi-lun, 102–04

Songchon River (North Korea), 11, 82–83, 86
Sonjagae-dong, North Korea, 43
Soule, MG Robert H. ("Shorty"), 67, 80, 96–97, 106
　awarded Distinguished Service Cross, 91
　command style, 23
　commands 3d Infantry Division, 21
　death of, 30 n.3
　early assignments, 21–23
　General Ridgway's opinion of, 23
　influence on junior officers, 23
　knowledge of CCF tactical doctrine, 76, 101–02
Soyang-ni, North Korea, 11
Stella, LTC Harry A., 26
Stilwell, GEN Joseph W. ("Vinegar Joe") 51, 59
Sudong, North Korea, 55, 70–71

Taebaek Mountains, 9, 12, 49
Task Force Charlie, 62–63
Task Force Dog, 25, 68, 70–71
Task Force Faith, 108, 110 n.11
Task Force Weyand, 66
Tientsin, China, 22
Togwon, North Korea, 40
Tokhung-ni, North Korea, 11, 46
Tokyo, Japan, 13, 17, 55, 106–07
Tomlinson, 1LT Jack, 24
Tonghung-ni, North Korea, 11, 80
Tongyang, North Korea, 42–43, 61, 65
Truman, President Harry S, 5
　commits ground forces in Korea, 7, 15
　meets MacArthur at Wake Island, 19

Unsan, North Korea, 55
USS *General William A. Mann* (AP 112), 21
USS *Missouri* (BB 63), 80, 92
USS *Mount McKinley* (AGC 7), 91, 95
USS *Rochester* (CA 124), 43, 80
USS *St. Paul* (CA 73), 80

Vancouver Barracks, WA, 22

Wake Island, 19
Walker, LTG Walton H., 15, 17, 105, 107
　death of, 109
　relationship with Generals Almond and MacArthur, 107–08
Washington, DC, 16–17, 55, 104
Weyand, LTC Fred C., 24–25, 66
Wonsan, North Korea, 9, 11, 12, 18, 40–41, 43, 45, 61–63, 65–66, 95

Yalu River, 54–55, 106–07
Yancey, LTC Thomas R., 25, 94
Yangdok, North Korea, 61
Yellow Beaches, 94
Yonghung, North Korea, 11, 41, 45, 62–63, 65–66
Yonghung Bay (North Korea), 9
Yonpo, North Korea, 11, 22
Yonpo Airfield, 11, 65, 76, 83
Yudam-ni, North Korea, 47, 56, 103–04